Praise for
A Long Walk Home

"*A Long Walk Home* pulls the reader through, particularly with a late scene that speeds the pulse. We learn how every violent taking of human life sends out ripples that last lifetimes. I found this mystery from my usually peaceful town fascinating."

—Tina Kelley, co-author of *Breaking Barriers: How P-TECH Schools Create a Pathway from High School to College to Career* and *Almost Home: Helping Kids Move from Homelessness to Hope*

"For those who like true crime but don't know this stretch of New Jersey, and for those who know New Jersey and don't read much true crime, here's a book that will satisfy your tastes—old and new."

—Marc Aronson, author of *Four Streets and a Square: A History of Manhattan and the New York Idea*

"Joe Strupp has an eye for stories that have gone mostly untold, an ear for the way the players in those stories might speak if given the chance, and the tools to bring those stories to light with heart and insight. *A Long Walk Home*, his account of a murder that has haunted his community for over fifty years, shines meaningful light on the life and death of a young woman whose murder has never been solved... True crime, well and truly told."

—Daniel Paisner, author of *A Single Happened Thing*

A Long Walk Home

A Long Walk Home

A young woman's unsolved murder and
her sister's lifelong search for answers

Joe Strupp

Author of *The Crookedest Street* and *Killing Journalism*

AMARNA
BOOKS & MEDIA
www.amarnabooksandmedia.com

ISBN: 978-1-7330875-5-1

Book design by Thomas Edward West of Amarna Books & Media. Photo of Joe Strupp by Joy Yagid

First print edition 2021

Amarna Books & Media
Maplewood, New Jersey

www.amarnabooksandmedia.com

For Carol Ann and Cynthia,
whose lives were disrupted forever.

For Cole, Cloey, and Claire.

Acknowledgements

I must thank Cynthia Farino for countless hours offering insight, details and stories of her journey and family information, photos and secrets. Thanks also to my dedicated and wonderful editor and publisher Thomas West of Amarna Books and Media.

For help with research, insight and information, thanks to Carl Malmquist, Vernon Geberth, Angela Caruso, Gabriela "Gabe" Bogden, Maggie Remigio, John Perna, Kevin Kisch, Beth Dircks, Barbara Payton, Ellen Fennessey, Bill Eisner, Beth Ward, Bill McGinnis Tommy Solomine Jane Tishman Scott Deitche, Marylou Bongiorno, Thomas A. McCabe, Connie A. Saindon, Bev Warnock, Anita Walls, Rod Leith, Fred Profeta, Bill Kuhl, Jr., and Peter Vronsky.

For support during research and writing and positive contributions, thanks to Tina Kelley, Marc Aronson, Daniel Paisner, Steve Seeman, Lou DeRossi, Sam Delson, Lauren Pacheco, and, always, Rick's front porch.

And, of course, to my family. First, my parents, James and Margo Strupp, who have always supported my work and helped me pursue my love of news and writing.

Last, but most important, thanks to my incredible wife, Claire, and my amazing children, Cloey and Cole, who put up with my time on the computer and the phone, my gripes about deadlines and headlines, and make my life the most it can be.

Table of Contents

Preface

I first heard of Carol Ann Farino after my wife, Claire, and I moved to Maplewood, New Jersey in late 2000.

After nine years in California, where Claire and I met, and 18 months living on the Upper East Side of Manhattan, we headed to the suburbs, with our first child on the way and eyes set toward buying our first house.

I was glad to return to the Garden State. I had spent my childhood in nearby Summit from age 6 through high school and college.

Three months after we moved into the home we still occupy on Yale Street, a grisly murder happened just six blocks away. Christine Burns, a local divorced mother of two, had been violently attacked and killed right in her front parlor.

As the news spread, the reporters who picked up the story kept noting it was only the second unsolved murder in Maplewood history.

The other one was Carol Ann Farino, who was killed way back in 1966.

Given that Maplewood's history begins in 1922 when it broke away from neighboring South Orange, it was not a long history at just 78 years.

Still, both murders in such a safe and friendly small town were frightening.

Burns's murder piqued my interest in 2000 because the Essex County Prosecutor's Office refused to reveal any information on possible suspects, or even say if they believed the killer was known to Burns.

For more than two years, the investigation continued without a hint at who might have slain the popular teacher and neighbor. Her former husband, who also lived in town, was quickly taken off the list when an alibi proved his innocence. She was also known to have frequented online dating sites, but no leads materialized.

Finally, in 2003, after nearly three years, I wrote a story for *New Jersey Monthly* on the case. A week later, officials announced that a man was arrested and charged with her murder.

He was an out-of-towner who had apparently chosen her house at random and rang the bell. When she answered, he attacked her and left her for dead. A new statewide DNA database was credited with finding him and he later pleaded guilty to aggravated manslaughter and aggravated sexual assault, receiving 20 years in prison.

Many in Maplewood breathed a sigh of relief.

Still, it left one unsolved murder in town.

A killing more mysterious, more perplexing, and perhaps more frightening than any other: the death of Carol Ann Farino, a 17-year-old high school student who was simply walking home one night and never made it. A pretty, young, popular girl whose life vanished too quickly, whose killer may well still be out there.

During the two decades we've lived in Maplewood, there have been 14 murders, the most recent a mentally ill son killing his mother in the town's only high-rise apartment building.

Others included a transgender woman shot to death in her home; a mentally disturbed young man who killed his father and grandmother, hid the bodies, and had a party; and three residents slain in an apparent drug deal gone wrong.

There was also a tragic love triangle in 2019 involving an au pair and her employer slain by a jealous ex-boyfriend.

In each case, the killers were found.

And in nearly all of them, Carol Ann Farino's name came up as the lone unsolved murder in town.

After a while I wanted to find out why.

Why did this innocent young woman die? Who could have executed such a violent crime? And why is it still unsolved?

Many cops in town still treat the case as a blemish on an otherwise stellar public safety record, while Carol's classmates and friends say they think of her often more than 50 years later.

Maplewood Police, meanwhile, have been extremely secretive in sharing information. Requests for a simple accounting of what has been done during the past five decades of investigation are met with blanket refusals and claims that it is an "active investigation."

The Essex County Prosecutor's Office, which actually controls the decision for any re-opening of the case or release of information, is even less helpful.

Then there is Carol's younger sister, Cynthia, who offered years of memories and pain that resulted from not only the loss of her only sibling, but the effect it had on her parents, her treatment by others, and her own struggle to go on.

She has also had her own battles with law enforcement over access to the files that might give her some hint as to who murdered her only sibling and how police appear to have failed in finding out.

Despite the opposition by many who are charged with tracking down the answers to Carol's death and providing her sister with some closure and relief, I believe we have uncovered enough of the story to offer what appears to be key answers to the questions of what happened and why.

And why has it remained unsolved for so long.

—Joe Strupp

Introduction

Cynthia Farino approached the apartment building in North Arlington, New Jersey, with hope and hesitation on a warm August day in 2020. The recently widowed woman had already had a rough year due to the Covid-19 outbreak and the death of her beloved husband, Michael, who lost a long battle with cancer just a few months earlier.

After more than 20 years of marriage, the couple had found a strong bond and connection that both had strived for during earlier trials and tribulations, which seemed to have thrown them together later in life for a much-needed coexistence.

But when he passed away during the worst pandemic of more than a century, Cynthia was not even able to give him a proper funeral or welcome well-wishers to her home just blocks from the Atlantic Ocean in the Jersey Shore's Monmouth County.

There was also the protracted battle with Michael's children from an earlier marriage over his funeral, last requests, and even money raised online to help with his final expenses. Cynthia's stepdaughter had refused to hand over the cash she had raised under the guise of paying his memorial bill.

Now Cynthia was set to meet a medium at the urging of a friend who knew she wanted to find some answers about Michael's final resting spot and perhaps other insights on their final years.

But she also had questions about the other close person in her life who had passed away decades earlier. Not someone who died as a senior citizen after a life well-lived. This was someone who was taken too young by a brutal killer who snatched away a promising future before it had a chance to be known.

Cynthia's sister, Carol Ann Farino, had been murdered nearly 54 years earlier at the age of 17. She died at the hands of an unknown killer who strangled her with her own stocking, tried to sexually attack her, and left her for dead in a dark, cold driveway.

The sisters lived with their parents in Maplewood, N.J., a small suburb about 20 miles north of the shore towns, at the time. Cynthia was less than 12 years old when it happened.

In the decades that passed, Cynthia continued to wonder who would have done such a thing as police turned up dead end after dead end in their investigation and her parents grew angrier, more guilt-ridden, and more lost in their despair.

For Cynthia, the killing not only took away her lone sister and close friend but stuck her with questions and a longing for answers that continued to this day. She had gone to psychics and mediums in the past but never got straight answers from those who may have been frauds.

But given the current year's events and conditions, she felt the need more than ever to seek some truths about that deadly night that still haunts her decades later.

When her friend suggested this medium, who seemed to have a way of knowing things about a subject without their name, background, or any hint of information, Cynthia was game for a try.

"I wanted to go because of Carol. Every time I went to a psychic in the past, I wasn't ready to hear anything, I would talk about problems I was having," she said. "This time I was really ready, I wanted to know stuff."

Maybe it was the loss of her husband and daily death updates on the Coronavirus; maybe it was feeling the freedom of reaching retirement age and letting her curiosity expand to something as unusual and perhaps misguided as clairvoyance; or maybe she was simply desperate enough for answers after facing more than five decades of unknowns to try anything.

"It is something that had been bothering me my whole life and not knowing it is a terrible feeling, always wondering what happened exactly and why they never found out who it was," she said. "I wanted to know because they made everybody think it was my dad, and when I realized it wasn't him, it was a mystery again and I didn't know who had done it."

Cynthia had many thoughts of Carol and Michael running through her mind as she climbed the steps to the medium's apartment building that Monday afternoon. Masked for proper virus protection, she had donned comfortable clothes—sneakers, leggings, and a white hoodie.

When she and her companion entered the apartment, she was struck by the spiritual décor and Native American elements placed about, including Indian artifacts, beads, and some feathered ornaments.

"As soon as I walked in the apartment, the sofa was right there, up against the wall so I sat down," Cynthia recalls.

The medium, an average-sized woman, entered and took a seat in a chair directly across from her visitors, but said nothing. Sporting dark clothes, large earrings, and long black hair, the purported visionary was straight out of central casting for a psychic, complete with a soft purring cat on her lap.

She even had a crystal ball on the table in front.

The medium then closed her eyes and leaned her head back, asking no questions or seeking any immediate information. She began to rub her own throat and look skyward.

"I was watching her and I thought, 'here it comes.'" Cynthia said.

"Then she said, 'Your sister was murdered and she was strangled, right?'"

Cynthia's eyes widened and she threw a glance at her friend as if to say, 'did you tell her that?' Her pal shot back a shaken head 'No' look and the two just glared at the spiritual impresario.

Then the woman said Carol was very secretive and had a secret life. Cynthia said she did not think so, that perhaps the woman was talking about herself, about Cynthia: "She said she was wild and I said you are talking about me."

"She saw [Carol] serving people and bending over a counter," a startling observation given that Carol had worked nights in a local diner and was last seen at a town eatery before her death.

"She was seeing her walk home and that somebody grabbed her and pulled her into a car," Cynthia said about the vision that mirrored what most investigators had suspected.

The woman continued for nearly two hours and was all business. As she sat in the chair, occasionally petting the cat whom she claimed gave her spiritual energy, she asked questions and shared visions that seemed to connect directly to Carol and Cynthia.

When it was over, Cynthia felt a spark of hope, but not enough to feel assured at knowing what happened or why.

"I felt good when I left, but I did not feel like I got enough out of that," she said. "It made me want to find out even more what happened. We are getting bits and pieces and I need to find out what the cops have, but they won't help. I have little strings of things that go nowhere."

Chapter One

The party at Beth Dircks' house was not supposed to be a big deal. The Columbia High School senior just wanted to take advantage of the long weekend that began that Thursday night in November 1966.

Thanks to the New Jersey Education Association, the statewide teachers' union, November 3 and 4 were set aside for the annual NJEA convention in Atlantic City.

That meant all teachers had those two days off, which meant each student did as well. So bring on the four-day weekend!

"I wasn't a party maker. If I had a party it was just come over to my house and we'll hang out, listen to music, and just talk," Dircks said years later. "Maybe five or six friends. That was it."

The high school senior was looking forward to a small but fun gathering as she put out the chips and soda and turned on the Beatles music.

"I also liked The Dave Clark Five, the Monkees, the Rolling Stones," Dircks recalled. "My sisters were into the Paul Ankas and Annette Funicellos. It was not a big thing."

But as the night went on, more people kept showing up to her house at 20 South Pierson Road, just up the hill from busy Valley Street and across from the Maplewood Country Club.

Word spread quickly in the small suburban town 20 miles west of Manhattan. Columbia High students wanted to start the long weekend early and a rare mid-week gathering was the perfect way to do it.

And the fact that the high school drew from both Maplewood and neighboring South Orange created a larger group of would-be guests tempted to crash the Dircks house.

"I didn't like having people coming to my house who weren't invited," Dircks said. "It was me at the door keeping people out. They were mostly people I knew from school, but some others just showed up and didn't come in. I was aware that there were people outside, but I didn't know who they were."

At one point her small gathering turned into a party that came close to being out of control, at least in her eyes, although never requiring police response.

"More people showed up with other people and it was bigger than I thought," Dircks, now a resident of Budd Lake, N.J., said. "I didn't like it with people crashing it. I didn't like it; I didn't want it."

One person who did not go to the Dircks house that night was Carol Ann Farino. The attractive, dark-haired, popular 17-year-old was working the counter at Milt's Cup and Saucer in Maplewood Village, the cozy downtown about a half-mile from South Pierson that spans all of four blocks and resembles something out of a German hamlet.

A senior at Columbia High School, Carol eschewed many of the late-night gatherings and juvenile events that would often lead to trouble, focusing on a steady job and small get-togethers with friends.

But she was not a home-bound hermit by any means. With a natural dark-eyed beauty and friendly smile, Carol sported the Jackie Kennedy-style hair of the day and what her sister called "a classic Italian nose," luring more than a fair share of interested young gentlemen callers.

She enjoyed high school dating and never had too many heartbreaking crushes, according to her sister, Cynthia. Her sibling recalled one time when a former boyfriend had come back into Carol's life, made a date with her, then stood her up at the last minute.

Carol's response: "Men are like buses, there's another one coming along every 10 minutes."

The elder of two sisters who had moved from neighboring Newark just three years earlier, Carol spent many weeknights on the job and often stayed to visit after work with other employees or the owner, Milton Miles, friends say.

On the night of November 3, she left Milt's at about 7:30 p.m. and stopped in at nearby George's Luncheonette, just a block away, to see her former boss there, George Mouhtis. She reportedly left there by 8 p.m., according to police. She was last seen between 8:05 p.m. and 8:10 p.m., police said.

Also working at George's that night was classmate Barbara Payton, a fellow senior who recalled seeing her: "Carol and I were both working that night, at two different places. I think she was walking home. She was friendly, she was a sweet, sweet girl."

Carol would routinely walk the half-mile from Milt's straight up Maplewood Avenue, the village's main street, then hang a right onto Jefferson Avenue to Number 5, the single-family house just a stone's throw from Valley Street.

She could also cut through nearby Memorial Park, Maplewood's two square blocks of greenery, fields, and foliage, and take the alternate route along Valley Street. Cutting through the park in those days was considered safe, although it lacked the hidden cameras that now surround the park and feed regular visuals to the police department.

"It was quiet, you wouldn't have any fear of anything. You could walk all over the place," Payton recalled years later. "It has always been a nice place. No fears of anything, the whole time growing up there. I walked everywhere."

But friends who sometimes walked with Carol said the direct route along Maplewood Avenue was the more common choice. While it was a busy, wide street with plenty of lights, an evening stroll in early November offered less sunlight than one might expect earlier in the year. Police said witnesses placed her walking north on Maplewood Avenue just after 8 p.m.

Either route would give the teenager limited protection and offer anyone who wanted to bother her more cover of darkness.

When she arrived home, Carol would usually work through homework and visit with friends on the phone. On the nights she worked, dinner was often provided by Milt's or George's. Still, her mother, Ann, would check if she was hungry.

Her father, Frank, the son of Italian immigrants, worked overnight hours as a delivery man for *The Star-Ledger*, New Jersey's largest newspaper. So by the next evening, he would be finished and kept tight tabs on Carol's whereabouts.

Both parents were strict and rarely let anyone in the house, said Cynthia. She said their father could be abusive and her mother often depressed.

"I remember him yelling and screaming at her because he found out she smoked," Cynthia recalled. "She didn't have any privacy, we didn't have a lot of privacy. They had to know every little thing we did, who we talked to, and where we were going."

But her parents had their good moments and stuck together, Cynthia remembers.

"He had a great sense of humor and if you met him you would think he is a great guy," she said of her father. "People loved him, they thought he was funny. My mother would egg him on."

"My father didn't have a lot of close, close friends; my mother didn't either. They had a few friends, and she played cards with a bunch of women."

Maplewood, then as now, had long been considered a safe and friendly community. At 25,000 residents today, it's not much more crowded than it was back in 1966 when the population reached nearly 24,000.

A less diverse town at that time, with mostly white, middle-class residents, the community had an image of being active and civic-minded, as well as a popular home for New York City transit commuters.

Violent crime and juvenile delinquency were no greater than in any other small suburban town. Still, Frank and Ann Farino did not want to take chances.

One of the reasons they moved from Newark's Vailsburg area was the growing concern over racial incidents and related clashes. While Vailsburg was a safe, friendly neighborhood, the '60s were creating increased tension over race, an increasingly unpopular war in Vietnam, and the sexual revolution.

But even in the new hometown, Carol and Cynthia's parents were adamant about keeping them in control and under a tight parental eye that also included concerns over any rebellious influence, especially in their older daughter.

Cynthia remembers her father tearing a Doors poster off Cynthia's bedroom wall and burning it in the back yard. "One time when she was playing 'I Think We're Alone Now' and my father ripped it off the record player and flung it against the wall, breaking it," she said.

Columbia High School dates back to 1815 in Maplewood when it began as a one-room schoolhouse located at Academy Street and South Orange Avenue in South Orange. A larger building was constructed on that site in 1879 and later expanded to a high school in 1885.

The school built its reputation as a place for innovation and ground-breaking teaching methods early on, with some of the first science curriculums in the state added in 1891, and musical enrichment two years later. The first girls' and boys' athletic teams were formed in the early 1900s, with a student council in 1912. *The Columbian* student newspaper that still operates today was launched in 1915.

"There was a reaction to these changes. Complaints arose over so-called 'fads and frills'—unessentials said to be leading to the neglect of reading, writing, spelling, and arithmetic," the school district's official history states. "New York papers read by local commuters campaigned for a return to the efficiency of the 'little old red schoolhouse.' But the changes were here to stay. At the same time, pupil behavior was becoming less inhibited, much to the distress of the adult population."

Henry W. Foster, superintendent from 1900-1927, described the conditions in 1913: "Long before prohibition was adopted, venturesome boys were surreptitiously now and then bringing liquor to dances to add to the excitement. There was a decided reversion to the animalistic excitement. Musical rhythm from the wilds of barbarism stirred the pulse. The dance abandoned the restraint and refinement of waltz and polka; Bunny Hug, Turkey Trot, Fox Trot, and Shimmy began to reign."

The Board of Education reacted by restricting all but "polite dances" on school premises, later banning them altogether for years.

In 1926, construction began on the present Columbia High School building at Valley Street and Parker Avenue, just two blocks from the Farino home. It opened in the fall of 1927.

Since then, the high school has boasted a history of creative programs and famed alumni—from Academy Award-winning actress Teresa Wright, a 1938 graduate, to pop star SZA, who received her diploma in 2008 under her given name, Solána Imani Rowe. In between, Columbia High School alumni have included actor Roy Scheider, actress Elisabeth Shue, musicians Max Weinberg and Lauryn Hill, and future *Miami Herald* publisher Alberto Ibarguen.

CHS is also credited with inventing Ultimate Frisbee, the soccer-like disc game created in the student parking lot in 1968.

"Maplewood was fun, innocent, we all had a great time," recalls Ellen Fennessey, another of Carol's CHS classmates. "There were no drugs at the time, the only thing was that people would go behind the school and have a Parliament cigarette. You could walk to Maplewood Village at night and with no fear. We would spend the whole period together talking and laughing, carrying on like young girls do."

"We used to go to Memorial Park, where a lot of kids would hang out after school and I would see [Carol] in town," Ellen said. "She was a very quiet girl, the kind of person you would have to seek out. In no way was she flamboyant. She did not put herself out there at all. Quiet, sweet, kind."

Ellen recalls Carol having to be home earlier than other friends and always aware of the time: "If we had to be home at 10, she had to be home at 9."

During their sophomore year, both girls were forced to sit out during the same gym class. For Ellen it was due to an arm injury, while Carol's was an unknown health-related issue.

When the other students played volleyball or did calisthenics, Carol and Ellen would sit in the upper bleachers that circled the first-floor girls' gymnasium and gossip like any teenage duo.

"I don't know why, we spent the whole class just talking," Ellen recalls. "She talked about wanting to be a nurse. Nothing very deep, girl stuff."

By the time Carol entered her senior year in the fall of 1966, Columbia was as transformed as any American high school, with rebellious songs and views being exchanged, long hair and colorful clothes trending, and the first hints of anti-war and civil rights chatter.

Students were well on their way to being more independent and outspoken than those from just a decade before.

"The whole cultural revolution was affecting Maplewood, too," said former Mayor Fred Profeta, a 1957 CHS graduate. "The culture changed, the kids were modeling themselves to look and act like the hippies. Kids were congregating in Memorial Park, which we didn't do in the 50s."

The 1967 yearbook was dedicated to the United Nations, while the 1966 version offered a plea for peace in the growing days of the Vietnam War.

"Above all, we wish to honor each man's lonely agony in his effort to affirm his beliefs that peace is not abstract or ephemeral," it said, in part. "That death in Vietnam is not without purpose; that 'man is really good at heart'…we hope that we may fulfill his optimistic expectations."

But the Class of 1967 also engaged in the typical high school events. *The Glass Menagerie* and *South Pacific* were the major student productions, while the football team posted a disappointing 2-6 record that year. Soccer coach Gene Chyzowych, in his fourth season, led the CHS varsity team to a weak 5-7-2 record.

But Chyzowych would go on to coach another 46 seasons and end up with one of the winningest high school coaching records in U.S. history: more than 750 victories on the way to a record-breaking 50 seasons as head coach before stepping down in 2013.

The school population remained an overwhelming white majority, with Carol's graduating class including just nine black students out of more than 600. That lack of diversity would change in the decades that followed, with CHS becoming a majority-minority school by the mid-1990s.

"I had 420 people graduating in my high school class, and 10 black kids," Profeta said. "It was white-dominated, everything was white."

Both South Orange and Maplewood remained safe communities during the 1960s, although the race riots of neighboring Newark just two months after the 1967 Columbia High graduation would spark concerns.

"The perception that there was very low crime was true," Profeta recalled. "It was very different. People wouldn't lock their doors."

He recalled going for joy rides in high school with friends who would find cars with the keys left in the ignition: "Any kind of crime of any magnitude came as a shock."

One of those shocks occurred in 1958 when two students set fire to the Maplewood Junior High School building, causing $300,000 worth of damage and shutting down the school for a week. But violent crimes such as rape, armed robbery, or murder were unheard of.

Still, Frank Farino practiced a strict form of parenting which meant neither of his daughters would get out much. "She had a real tight leash on her from her father," Ellen Fennessey says of Carol. "She sort of portrayed him as the old-fashioned Italian father."

But Carol's friends and neighbors don't recall her ever complaining about her strict upbringing, although it was clear that her busy work schedule, school commitments, and time with friends were ways to avoid facing the home life demands.

"We used to hang out [at Milt's] while she was working," said Bill Eisner, a fellow senior who met Carol just a few months earlier. "I would talk to her on the phone a lot at the time. That was a thing, that she didn't get out much."

Eisner, who lived about five blocks from the Farino house on quiet Euclid Avenue, recalls Carol's upbeat attitude and her hopeful plans for life after graduation: "She was the best, she never hurt anybody or had a mean thing to say. She was a good person. She wanted to do something caring, like social work or advanced nursing."

Fellow senior Beth Ward echoed that view: "She was a doll, a sweet, shy, simple girl. That is the best description. I knew her from classes and socializing. We ended up in Maplewood Village or South Orange."

Ward said meeting most of the large senior class was not difficult because students went to a lot of the same places, in and out of school.

"It was socializing in the hallways, at lunch, we had a long table with a ton of people," she said. "The classes were all close, you could be friends with everybody. Everyone was pretty decent, pretty easy-going."

Ward recalls dances at the community house in South Orange and regular gatherings inside and outside of Gruning's, the popular ice cream parlor that had two locations along busy South Orange Avenue.

But she also recalls Carol's participation was limited.

"She worked a lot. We never worked. That was a whole thing because she would not be available," Beth Ward said. "Her dad was pretty strict. I knew her well but not well enough to see why her father would allow it or not. She did work and a lot of us did not."

One school group Carol apparently had time for was the Personality Club, an odd band of about a half-dozen girls who managed to get a spot in the yearbook, with the description of "[a] secret organization of junior and senior girls." It also said the group was "...composed of the most select girls, its objective to prepare them for life in our keenly competitive world and to become young women of tomorrow."

The yearbook photo of the "club" with buckets and mops lends credence to its less-than-serious mission.

"I knew her pretty well; we did not mix in the same circles of friends, but we were pretty friendly anyway, I liked her," Beth Dircks said. "She was a nice girl and I was attracted to that. We were friendly in school and I knew that she had the job and I saw her one day walking in Maplewood Village, to or from work."

But Dircks recalls Carol's willingness to walk alone, even in the dark: "I had mentioned to her that she walked to work alone, we didn't think that was dangerous in Maplewood. You are taught not to walk around by yourself and I knew when she was working it was at night."

Fellow senior Bill McGinnis—who lived two houses from the Farinos on Jefferson Avenue—worked at a Maplewood Village grocery and would often walk home with Carol.

"I would walk up the hill and we walked the half-mile or so the same route," he said, noting he was off work the night of November 3. "We generally came home about 7 or something from our jobs. I did not know her friends, but she was so nice all the time and easy to talk to. I wasn't very social at the time and it was easy to talk to her and I enjoyed walking home and having her right there."

One of the reasons Carol did not plan to go out the evening of November 3, 1966, was Tommy Solomine, her older boyfriend who had failed to call earlier in the week to make plans for the long weekend, her sister remembers.

"She was upset that day because she had not heard from him," Cynthia Farino recalled. "She was probably hoping to get home and wait for his call. But I think she liked him more than he liked her."

Despite her parents' tight control over their socializing, Cynthia said they knew about Tommy and never tried to break them up, even though he was three years older.

"It was not unusual back then for girls to go out with older boys," Cynthia said about the young man who had graduated from Columbia High School three years earlier. He later joined the U.S. Army and would attend Carol's funeral in his military dress uniform, she said.

By his own admission, Tommy Solomine was "[a] little wild." A Harley-Davidson biker, he also played bass in a local pop band, The Fairlanes, which had minor success with a few singles in later years, among them one titled "Little Girl, Little Girl."

"They wanted to make sure who I was and what my intentions were," Solomine recalls about Carol's parents. "A typical Italian father. They didn't mind me and I was surprised. We dated and when we were dating I was in the service."

After graduating from CHS in 1964, Tommy entered the high school's post-graduate program in 1965, then joined the Army later that year. When he met Carol through a friend in the summer of 1966, he was stationed at Fort Meade, Maryland, but would return to Maplewood often.

"I had been coming home on the weekends, get those weekend passes. We would go out," he recalled. "She was a very pleasant girl, hard-working. Very nice. The kind of girl you enjoyed and had a good time with."

He remembers spending a lot of time at a community center in South Orange where dances were held, some that included his band, along with shooting pool.

"We used to go to the dances and we had only gone out for a few months. We would go to the Maplewood Theater for movies, too," he said. "It wasn't a long relationship, but it might have become one."

Tommy recalled Frank Farino as an intimidating but accepting man: "I remember then asking about her father because he was a strong man at the time. He did a lot of lifting and had real muscular arms."

Expecting to be sent to Vietnam at some point in his three-year Army tenure, Tommy said it never happened, in part because the colonel who oversaw him at Fort Meade wanted him to remain there.

"I got orders for overseas, for Vietnam, but my boss at Fort Meade was a colonel and his boss was a general and they wanted me to stay, they got me off of two sets of orders."

Tommy Solomine was not the only older man Carol dated in high school. Fellow CHS classmate Sandra Wujciak remembers setting Carol up with a friend of her college boyfriend a year earlier. John Little, from Mountain Lakes, N.J., was attending St. Francis College in Maine with Sandra's beau.

"We set up the date, it was only one date, but she was personable, a good conversationalist, so we had fun," Sandra said. The foursome went to dinner in nearby Union, then for ice cream after at Jaan's, a favorite hangout at the time.

"We had double-dated a few times," Sandra recalled. "She enjoyed working at the luncheonette; she was the type that could make friends easily, a good girl. All I can remember is that I wanted to go to work after graduating high school and I think Carol did, too."

After a long shift at Milt's that November night in 1966, Carol would likely have reached out to her close friend, Katharine "Kitty" Maher, especially if she was brooding over Tommy's failure to call. Known for her friendly support to classmates, the Columbia High School yearbook, *The Mirror*, that year called Kitty the "Ann Landers of Columbia."

"To my very best favorite friend in the world," Kitty had written in Carol's junior year annual just six months earlier. "It seems to me that I have never been so close to one person. I have never met anyone with such insight and one so sensitive. I'll always need and want your friendship. I'll never forget the good and bad times, the tears and joys and heartbreaks. All the luck in the world and all my love."

Bill Eisner said the three of them were close those last few months: "Kitty and Carol and I were really good friends, we were a trio."

Kitty, who later married and became Katharine Eckelkamp, died in 2005.

Then there was Jane Tishman, Carol's other close friend who lived across the street from 5 Jefferson Avenue. On her way home that night, Carol may well have planned to stop in to see her neighbor or ask her to come over to commiserate about school, boys, and work.

"She moved to Maplewood to start high school and I met her the first day. We became fast friends because we lived so close," Jane recalled. "My parents worked nights so I would hang out at her house because I did not want to be alone. We were as close as you could imagine for a few years. I basically lived there for years. Her mother was just the kindest person. She taught me how to make gravy one time, I recall."

Jane and Carol had both initially worked together at George's Luncheonette. "One night I came in and Carol was going to work that night and I switched with her. Then she got a job working at Milt's," Jane remembered. "We went through all the same things that girls in high school go through, we hung out in the same groups. We were teenage girls, we did our hair together, we ran through the magazines together, we had a lot of fun."

Jane Tishman was born in and grew up in the Inwood section of upper Manhattan, but her family moved to Maplewood a few years before the Farinos arrived. Jane's mother had gotten a job doing promotion at the nearby Paper Mill Playhouse in Millburn.

"My mother thought it would be a safer place to live," Jane said, noting her mother eventually worked on Broadway productions, a career Jane later followed. "I think she was looking out for our best interests, in retrospect."

She recalls that senior year with Carol and others as a positive time, at least for the first few months.

"It was the beginning of our senior year and we had just had our pictures taken for the yearbook," she remembers. "We had started to date and I had a serious boyfriend, so we did not spend a lot of time together. But we were such good friends."

"We went to dances, we hung out after school. I would have dinner there very often, a lot. Probably five nights a week and they accepted me into their house and they were lovely people. We came from different worlds, but we were thrown together. We just wanted to go out and have fun and have a handsome boyfriend, get married, and have children."

Neither Kitty, Sandra, Bill, Beth, Tommy, or Jane spoke to Carol the night of November 3. As she left George's Luncheonette that Thursday evening, it was the last time anyone who knew her would see her alive.

She had one last task before heading home, dropping off a bill at the

Maplewood Post Office, located just down the street from Milt's. Her boss had asked her to put the PSE&G utility payment in the mail on her way home. As usual, Carol gladly obliged.

Maplewood Village was unusually busy for a weekday night, due in part to the closed school days that gave many youngsters an excuse to go out for the evening.

The local Democratic Committee was holding a fundraiser at the Maplewood Theater, less than two blocks from Milt's. A ticket-taker later told police she recalled Carol walking past the theater at around 8 p.m. that night.

A stock boy at nearby Kings Market, a few feet from the theater, noticed Carol passing by as well while he worked on his stalled car. The boy told investigators he recognized Carol but did not offer her a ride because of the car trouble. A lie detector test later confirmed his statements.

Since Carol had walked from Milt's north on Maplewood Avenue, past the theater and the market, she was likely planning to stay on the avenue rather than cut through Memorial Park. Her most likely route would have been to stroll along the busy roadway until she reached Jefferson Avenue, turned right, and walk the last long block home.

But she never made it.

Chapter Two

Ann Farino started to get worried about her older daughter at around 8:30 p.m. on the night of November 3. She knew Carol had gotten off work an hour earlier, and even with a stop off on the way home she would have normally been back by then.

Or she would have at least called, knowing her parents' strict rules and penchant for concern. By 8:45 p.m. Ann had had enough and asked her youngest daughter, 11-year-old Cynthia, to wake her father and ask him to go out looking.

"I did not think it was so late, I wondered why she was so nervous," Cynthia recalls. "I was still dressed so it couldn't have been too late. I had to get my father from bed, which took a couple of times because he did not want to get up."

After nearly 20 years, Ann and Frank Farino had seen the wear and tear of life on their marriage. Dealing with the stresses of the '60s, which would only worsen in the coming years, the couple also took the raising of their two daughters seriously, and harshly.

At 46, Ann was battling middle age depressions and demands. She often wondered about how her life might have gone a different way if she had met someone else.

Living with a husband who could fly off the handle at a moment's notice, often blaming her and their children for the troubles of the day, was difficult.

"My father would lose his temper and I did not like him at all," Cynthia said. "He hit me more; I was never close with my father, my sister was when she was little. Their relationship was better when they had her. By the time they had me they were going downhill."

Cynthia was lying on the living room rug watching television when her mother's worry sparked the request to get her father up and out searching that night. The TV choices that night ranged from *F Troop* and *The Munsters* to *Alfred Hitchcock Presents* and *Star Trek*.

A more outspoken child than her sister, Cynthia was the one who would counter her mother and father's orders or restrictions more than her older sibling.

In her first year at Maplewood Junior High School, the seventh-grader saw how her parents kept Carol down and ruled with an iron hand, making both daughters fearful of stepping out of line and unable to enjoy most of the teenage fun of the era.

"I felt like I wasn't going to die without experiencing things. I became sneaky and wasn't going to put up with that," Cynthia said years later. "Carol was easy to control, she never really fought back and she let them treat her that way. She kind of went along with it; she was never angry and upset. I was angry for her."

When her mother asked Cynthia to awaken her father, she went up to the room where he was sleeping but knew it would not go over well. Frank Farino kept an early schedule due to his newspaper delivery job that had him out at just after midnight and home when everyone else was having breakfast.

Cynthia also felt that she would somehow be blamed for this disturbance to his rest, that he was always taking things out on her more than her sister or mother. That might have caused her rebellious response. By the time he had a second child, Frank seemed less than interested in the responsibilities.

"I was sickly with asthma and allergies," Cynthia said. "He would not go to the drug store to get my medicine while I would have an asthma attack. He would finally get up and go to the store after a while, but it took a lot and I was suffering."

It didn't help that Ann Farino never learned to drive, forcing her husband to do all of the tasks that required a car—from shuttling the girls around to running errands and spearheading long drives.

Frank stood shorter than most men, at about five feet, two inches tall. A year older than his wife, he sported a rugged Italian look, with salt and pepper hair and a grin that could charm others when he chose to.

But his temper was on display as well, and not confined just to Cynthia. She recalled times when he would take it out on his firstborn as well—sometimes physically and violently.

"When he caught her smoking somewhere one time, probably down in Maplewood Village, I remember he got mad and came home to wait for her," Cynthia recalled. "He was waiting for her to come home, they had a big argument and he threw her out the back door."

Frank had been asleep a few hours when Cynthia went upstairs to do as her mother had asked that Thursday night. Cynthia was afraid to even enter his bedroom, wanting to avoid an angry reaction. Experience taught her that getting too close would spark an argument.

"I would stand by the doorway and say, 'Dad, you have to get up, Dad! Get up!' It would take a while," she said. "It was brutal to try and get him up. He was always cranky and tired because he didn't like to be woken up."

Frank's first reaction was to snap at her for interrupting his sleep. But when Cynthia told him Carol had yet to return, Frank's response was more annoyance than worry. He pulled himself out of bed and headed downstairs.

"I don't know why she wouldn't call for a ride, she probably knew that he would get angry if he had to drive her," Cynthia recalls thinking at the time. "I blamed him. It just pissed me off so bad the way he would act toward her. My mother for years blamed him as well, that if he had picked her up nothing would have happened."

As he exited the house onto the quiet of Jefferson Avenue, Frank felt the November chill on the clear night and closed up his coat before lumbering into the car. Ann and Cynthia peeked out the window hoping that he would find the delayed older daughter. Ann's worry only intensified.

The youngest of nine children, Ann Farino, formerly Ann Luciani, was born and raised in Newark and met her husband prior to his U.S. Army service in World War II. The oldest of three brothers, Frank also grew up in Newark.

Cynthia recalls the couple often fighting and her mother appearing stressed and almost sad and angry at the marriage.

"My mother came from a loving family, but my father was abusive, verbally abusive, physically abusive. He had a terrible childhood," Cynthia said. "His parents were Italian immigrants, his father was an alcoholic who beat his mother and the kids."

At about the same time Frank Farino was cruising through Maplewood and South Orange in search of his daughter, Jane Tishman was enjoying the rare weeknight off with friends outside Gruning's Ice Cream Shop in South Orange.

The old-fashioned hot fudge sundae emporium was legendary in the area then, dating back to 1925 when the German immigrants who opened the first shop in Harlem expanded into the suburbs. From the 1940s to the 1970s, Gruning's was the hangout spot for CHS students with two locations in town, the other at the top of South Orange Avenue.

Many nights the crowd would spill out into the Gruning's parking lot, which became an instant meet-up spot for local youngsters just wanting a place to congregate.

Frank Farino made the hot spot one of his first visits during the search, spotting Jane and then approaching her anxiously.

On that cool Thursday night, Jane was chatting it up with several friends among a large crowd when Frank came to her with a worried look on his face.

"Everybody was milling around there and her father walked up to me and was relieved to see me," Jane recalls. "He asked if I had seen Carol and he said he had been looking for her and couldn't find her. I told him I hadn't seen her.

"He asked if I wanted to come and look for her with him, but I didn't. I wanted to stay with my friends and he said it was okay, but I could see the look of disappointment on his face that I wouldn't get in the car to look for her. I know the track she would walk home that night, it was very, very cold, it was a really miserable time that night."

With that, Frank sped off wondering where else to find his first-born child and noticing that time was getting later and later.

As Frank continued his search, Beth Ward was leaving the party at Beth Dircks's house and heading back toward South Orange. The group she was driving with happened to pass the Farino home on Jefferson after 10 p.m. and noticed the family was still up.

"We were out riding around after the party and I remember driving by her house and someone saying the porch light is still on," Ward remembered. "And someone said her father always left the light on until Carol came home."

Soon after that, Frank Farino returned to update his family, all of whom became more and more concerned that Carol had yet to appear.

"He came home after he went out the first time and that's when he got worried," Cynthia recalled. "He said he couldn't find her and my mother said he should go to the police. When he went he was scared."

As Frank left again, Ann Farino hit the telephone, calling anyone who might know Carol's whereabouts. She tried to keep a calm voice, but whoever answered those calls could tell she was frightened.

Among them was Carol's close friend, Kitty Maher.

When Ann told Kitty that Carol was still not home, it prompted Kitty to head out on her own search, taking their friend, Bill Eisner, with her.

"Kitty called me and said Carol had not come home from work. She wanted to go check her walking route," Bill remembered. "When Carol didn't show up we went out looking for her until midnight."

Bill and Kitty went searching for hours in his 1956 Volkswagen but to no avail.

"It was two to three hours, riding around getting our hopes up. 'What is up?' we thought. Was she kidnapped?" Bill recalled. "We tooled around a little looking for her, around the train station and toward her house because that is the way she had gone home."

But none of the searches ever resulted in Carol being found alive.

When Frank Farino reached Maplewood Police headquarters, it was sometime between 10 and 11 p.m. The small, brick building on quiet Dunnell Road stood across from Memorial Park, the same center of activity where Carol and hundreds of other township teens would congregate after school and on weekend nights.

The park had been created as a center of public service when the township was designed with the town hall, train station, fire department, public library, recreation center, and, of course, the police department, all built to circle the parcel of land. It also held memorials to Maplewoodians who died in each war since World War I.

This cold evening there was still a small group gathered to enjoy the night off. But Frank was not concerned with them. He had to go in and report his daughter missing.

Still tired from his shortened sleep, Frank approached the small brick building that would later be considered too cramped and outdated for 21st Century policing and see the wrecking ball to make way for a new apartment complex on the parkside site. Police activities were relocated to a larger, modern facility across town on Springfield Avenue.

But on this night, the aging police station was the focus of Frank's task. The wind blew cold as he opened the heavy front door and walked in, turning right toward the main desk and loosening his jacket.

The hallway was quiet as soft light paved the way for Frank to approach the desk officer, who raised his head. Just as Frank reached the counter, his eyes glanced behind the patrolman and scanned the room. There were wanted signs and police notices, along with a clock, filing cabinets, and an American flag in the corner.

Then he saw it.

An item that stopped Frank Farino in his tracks.

A chill went up his spine and his eyes opened wide. There, on a chair next to the sergeant was a piece of clothing all too familiar to the father of two.

Just as a parent knows their child's smile, their favorite toy, and even their handwriting, Frank Farino recognized this item. A warm, winter jacket that he'd seen dozens of times before that fall.

The dark blue ladies' car coat had kept his daughter warm on many a chilly day and was usually the last thing she put on before going out in the current climate.

He knew the coat was Carol's.

And he knew what it meant.

About two hours earlier, Vincent J. Vaccarella and his wife, Dolores, were leaving their home at 22 Sommer Avenue, just a block east of Valley Street in Maplewood. The couple was on their way out to the big Democratic Committee fundraiser at the Maplewood Theater that night, the same one that Carol had passed less than an hour earlier.

The Vaccarellas were running late as the hour approached 8:45 p.m. and they hustled to their driveway, which faced the quiet side street of Hubert Place and ran perpendicular to Sommer, stretching all of one block.

As Vincent and Dolores reached their car, they noticed a dark object in the corner of the driveway, placed under a large tree next to the garage. At first glance, it looked like the body of a boy.

The sight of the apparently lifeless person startled them both and they approached it slowly. Dolores did not want to go near it, but Vincent eased his way forward. He stopped short and decided they'd better call the police.

Around the same time, a neighbor across the street on Hubert Place noticed the same thing and telephoned the cops. She, too, mistook the person for a boy, perhaps due to the darkness, and reported it as such. But she dared not venture out.

When police arrived, they discovered it was actually a girl.

They later confirmed it was Carol Ann Farino.

Police reports described her body as being found face up in the corner of the driveway at the base of a large tree. She still had her white waitress uniform on, but her stockings had been removed and one was tied tightly around her neck. It was later assumed she had been strangled with her own hosiery as her legs were bare.

Carol's shoes were missing and her uniform was open in front, with her underwear described as "not disturbed," but her girdle down around one ankle. There was no apparent sign of sexual assault, although investigators would later theorize that her killer had possibly planned to rape or assault her but stopped before he could finish.

At the end of the driveway lay Carol's blue car coat, the same one that would startle Frank Farino just a few hours later at police headquarters.

In total, four patrolmen and one reserve officer responded to the scene. Among them was Patrolman Anthony Surano, who administered mouth-to-mouth resuscitation. Two other patrolmen, James O'Dowd and James Waddell, carefully cut the stocking from Carol's neck.

The officers attempted to revive her as it appeared she might be alive since her body was still warm. It would turn out she had been attacked less than an hour earlier.

Police would not give up hope, radioing in for an ambulance that arrived within minutes and brought paramedics who tried to administer oxygen to the young, brutally victimized teen.

But all efforts failed.

Carol Ann Farino was pronounced dead by Dr. John Evans, a police physician, at 9:07 p.m., less than an hour after she was last seen in Maplewood Village.

Her murder shocked the Vaccarellas, the officers involved, and eventually the entire community. Within minutes of her death being confirmed, those on the scene launched into the biggest manhunt in township history, a search that is still technically going on today.

They knew very little about who they were seeking, other than it was someone brazen enough, vicious enough, and cruel enough to kill an innocent young woman with their bare hands.

It had to be someone who could subdue her and from all signs of the crime, lure her into his or her vehicle as it appeared she showed no signs of a struggle or of having been forcibly moved. Her uniform was clean, with no rips, tears, or stains and her body had no cuts, bruises, or injuries other than deep strangulation marks on her neck.

Patrolman Raymond McConnell, one of those initial responders, recalled in his report seeing Carol just hours earlier during his own visit to George's Luncheonette, and remembered what he described as a "tall male in his 20s with red hair and a slight mustache."

McConnell also knew Barbara Payton and recalled that she worked at George's. When he asked her about it later that night, she confirmed seeing the mystery red-headed man, but did not know his name.

But the patrolman's immediate reaction after Carol's death was similar to his fellow officers on the case, spreading out for an immediate search of the area and issuing a bulletin to other cops in Maplewood and elsewhere that such a crime had occurred.

Patrolman Surano began a house-to-house search for clues and any witnesses and found one resident two doors down on Sommer Avenue who had been walking her dog just after 8:15 p.m. The neighbor said she had seen a man walking west on Sommer Avenue at about that time, and later heard a car with a bad muffler driving by.

But no suspects were found in the area.

Hours later, back at the Maplewood Police Headquarters, Frank Farino was coming to grips with the reality of the evening. His eldest daughter, an innocent, beautiful, friendly girl, was gone. More shocking and devastating was how she died—at the hands of a vicious killer who murdered her with her own stocking and left her to die in a dark, side street gasping for life.

Detective John Heffernan had broken the news to Frank at just about the time he planned to visit the Farino house to let them know Carol's body had been found. Sadly, Frank had one more gruesome task: to identify Carol's body that had been taken to a morgue in nearby Orange.

Heffernan—a veteran Maplewood officer who would go on to head the state Policeman's Benevolent Association (PBA)—drove Frank to the mortuary where Carol's body was being held. Heffernan was present as the mortuary workers uncovered her remains so Frank could see them. Once he completed the task, the detective drove him home so the two of them could break the news to Ann Farino.

When the duo entered the Jefferson Avenue house, it was well after 11 p.m. Cynthia had fallen asleep on the couch, but Ann was awake and more frantic than ever. She'd been on the phone for hours trying to track her daughter down. When she saw Frank with a police officer, she knew the worst was at hand and sat down slowly in a chair.

Frank comforted his wife as more police arrived to begin the grim task of trying to piece together what had happened and why. Everyone knew when Carol had left Maplewood Village, but what happened afterward was a frustrating void.

Her family was sure she had not reached home. But how far had her apparent walk taken her? Several of the police fanned out in the Farinos' neighborhood to see if any neighbors had seen her that night. If she had at least reached Jefferson Avenue, that would narrow down when she met her abductor and where.

"That night, I remember the police knocked at the door and had been going down the street asking if anyone had seen her," recalls Bill McGinnis, Carol's classmate who lived two houses away from her. "Everything was turned upside down, because someone doesn't just disappear in Maplewood, or on our street."

Bill Eisner did not get home from his search with Kitty Maher to his family's Wyoming Avenue house a few blocks west of the Farino home until after midnight and went straight to bed. He assumed Carol would be found and perhaps had already made her way home and to bed herself.

But at 2 a.m., he and his family got a rude awakening when police knocked on the door with the bad news and plenty of questions.

"The police woke me up and told me what happened. It was a real shock. The end of youth a little bit," Bill recalled years later. "They told me that she had died, and they had a few questions. That is not something you wanted to hear when you are 17 years old."

A month later, Bill's family would suffer its own strange abduction when his brother, Pete, was grabbed from a phone booth near the Maplewood train station, thrown into a car, and tied up with duct tape.

"A guy came up with a gun and said, 'get in the car,'" Bill explained. "He taped his hands together and my brother got the door open and rolled out of the car and got away." That perpetrator was never found, either.

The most shocking and sad surprise might have been for young Cynthia Farino. Carol's younger sister, just 10 days away from her 12th birthday, was deep in slumber on the living room couch when the cops appeared to tell her mother that her first-born daughter had been murdered.

Cynthia was startled awake by the commotion of police, crying sounds, phone calls, and knocks at the door.

"When I woke up, there were cops all over the house, it was noisy and my mother was sitting in a chair, she was in shock. She wasn't crying, she was just in shock," Cynthia remembers. "I think it was one of the cops who told me. I think he was sitting next to me on the couch and he told me. I didn't cry, I was just in shock."

It may have seemed like a dream at first. When Cynthia fell asleep, all that was heard was the sound of the television and the quiet of the street outside. But once she was awake, Jefferson Avenue had turned into a swirl of activity with police cars blocking the street, officers roaming the sidewalk and knocking on doors, and neighbors wondering what had happened.

"My father was on the phone calling all of my relatives to tell them what happened and he was crying hysterically," Cynthia said. "I couldn't grasp what was going on, it didn't sink in right away. It was a crazy thing to wake up to."

At one point, Cynthia said Carol's Godparents—her Aunt Rose and Uncle Ernie from Colonia, N.J.—showed up and added to the hysteria. Rose, Ann's sister, seemed more upset and uncontrollable than Cynthia's mother.

"She just was on the floor, hysterical," Cynthia recounted. "At one point she needed a shot just to get control of herself, they called a doctor to do it."

Ann Farino began to break down, crying and feeling the guilt parents of deceased children often undergo, deserved or not. She unburdened herself a bit on Cynthia, saying her last conversation with Carol had been an argument that day.

"They had a huge fight, my mother kept saying she had a fight with her," Cynthia recalled. "Going on and on that they had a fight, but I don't know about what."

All of this for a young girl who had just started seventh grade, whose biggest worry should have been which 45's to play on her record player or how to dress to get the right boy to notice her.

Just a few hours earlier, Cynthia Farino was living the life typical of any pre-teen: excited and nervous about growing up, anxious for a long weekend of friends and fun, and curious about what the future would bring.

But in the span of just one evening, that outlook and optimism were destroyed for good. Instead, she would undergo the worst few days of her life and be forced to brace for a very different future.

Chapter Three

The police woke Beth Dircks up early on the morning of November 4, 1966. The night before had been quite a hassle with so many uninvited guests crashing her small gathering.

By midnight it became nearly out of control and finally came to an end shortly after 1 a.m. Then the clean-up took more time and when she finally went to bed she was exhausted, and a bit annoyed.

So when the cops came knocking on the door shortly after 8 a.m., it was an unexpected disturbance. Especially during what should have been a morning to sleep in with no school and a long weekend ahead.

When the investigators told her the tragic news of Carol's brutal murder, it startled her out of any grogginess from her previous night's slumber. Surprise and fear followed.

"It was very shocking. I was sad and upset," Beth remembers. "I liked her and was friends with her in school and if I saw her after school, we would hang out."

Then an even bigger fact emerged. Police were at her house because Carol had been found just two streets away. The Dircks House, at 20 South Pierson Rd., was a mere two blocks from the spot on Hubert Place where Carol's lifeless body had been left.

A few quick turns in a car or a two-minute stroll through some backyards and the killer could have easily made it to the party within minutes of the murder. And given the swarm of unknown guests, he or she could have blended in easily, police told Beth.

That just left her frozen.

"I had that thought for a while, for years, that somebody could have been at my house who was the person who murdered Carol," Beth recalled. "I tried not to dwell on it."

Police had the same thought and wanted to know everything about the night's activities: who came, when they came. And when they left. Also, if anyone looked suspicious.

"The police were all business; there were two of them and they were just asking questions, looking for information," Beth remembered, still upset about the events. "They were concerned because I had had an activity the night that she had died. They were asking me about the people because they were looking for more leads, that it might have been someone who had been at my house."

Other interviews with friends and classmates who had also been at the party had led investigators to Beth's, due in large part to few other clues. The initial case lacked two of the three required pieces of evidence usually needed to find and convict a killer: a witness, a confession, and a murder weapon.

Since Carol had been strangled by her own stocking, which was left behind, they had one of the three clues. But it was difficult to track it to the murderer since it was her own piece of clothing. Finding fingerprints from stockings can be difficult, although any hairs the killer might have dropped or other evidence that clung to the stocking could be valuable.

Police records do not say more about the personal items. DNA, meanwhile, was not the evidentiary breakthrough at the time that it would become years later.

"They wanted to know if I knew who was at the party. Could I tell them who my friends were?" Beth explained. "But there were some people I didn't even know. They were friends of friends. I gave them a few names of people I did remember, but I was not too helpful."

She said knowing the body was found so close made her shudder and wonder if the person could still be in the area.

"Who knows what people do with their sick minds? It was two blocks away," she said. "They had to ask and get as much information as they could. I couldn't believe it when we heard that she was strangled with her stocking. I never had any more parties after that."

The cops kept Beth, her parents, and her brother busy with questions for more than an hour, while fellow officers spread out across the small town looking for clues, any traces of a killer that no one else had seen, and anything that other classmates could tell them about what might have happened and the young girl whose life had been snuffed out.

Each person interviewed that day would lead to two or three more people to question, as friends as well as classmates who barely knew Carol offered up suggestions, theories, and, in some cases, simple guesses.

"I was at home the night it happened after work and the police came to my house the next day," recalls Barbara Payton, Carol's co-worker who was one of the last to see her alive. "The police came to my house to question me. They said she was found in the driveway and strangled. They asked a lot of questions. I had no ideas. I was shocked."

Once the police began knocking on doors and informing Columbia High School students and their frightened parents what had happened in their quest for information, the rumors and sad facts spread quickly throughout Maplewood and South Orange.

In the age before cell phones, Facebook, or email, it didn't take long for such a horrible story to work its way through phone channels and word of mouth. Each telling of the deadly tale ended with the same unknown: who could have done this?

And will they do it again?

"It was that telephone chain, everybody calling everybody else. And then it was in the paper," recalls Beth Ward, another classmate who had been at the Dircks party. "I remember it seemed like they questioned almost every boy who had anything to do with anything. It was very scary. Who knew what was going on?"

Fellow senior Ellen Fennessey said she got a call Friday morning, as many classmates did, from a friend breaking the news to her. With no school again that day, the phone calls came fast and furious, and early.

"My friend had called me that day, the next morning and said they found her strangled. It was beyond belief," Ellen said. "We lived in an innocent place, we never locked our doors or our cars. It was just be-yond belief."

Both Associated Press and United Press International had short sto-ries that morning with the basics on Carol, the time and place, and the most gripping fact: the unknown killer was still at large. The wire stories ran in most North Jersey newspapers.

The afternoon *Newark Evening News*, which had more time to put together a Friday story than its counterpart, the morning *Star-Ledger,* made it a front-page bombshell. Headlined: "Maplewood Girl, 17, Is Found Strangled," the story had all of the grisly details and Carol's year-book photo, along with a picture of the driveway where she was found.

Inside, the paper offered a side story interview with the owner of Milt's, who described Carol as "a hard worker" but "a loner." It also ran a photo of an unidentified friend leaving Maplewood police after being questioned and a detailed map showing the location of Carol's home, George's Luncheonette, and the spot where her body was found.

The local weekly—*The News-Record*—had to wait nearly a week for its next Thursday edition to report anything on the Maplewood crime of the year.

Throughout the morning and afternoon, as police blanketed the town with questions and searches, residents passed along the news in coffee shops, at bus stops and in the usual gathering locations.

At Milt's Cup and Saucer and George's Luncheonette, it was Topic A as police included their owners and workers in the long list of interview-ees, while customers could not help but guess at the cause and suspect who might have done this to one of their own.

"I was crying and crying and crying," Jane Tishman, Carol's friend from across the street, remembers. "A lot of crying. You try to ignore it and deny it. That is how I got through it at the time."

The initial approach by police was to speak to as many classmates as possible and then get a handle on Carol's private life.

That, of course, led to Tommy Solomine.

Carol's older boyfriend at 20, Tommy had been seeing her for just a few months during his U.S. Army stint and was at Fort Meade, Maryland, the night she died, giving him a clear alibi.

"I was the number one suspect because I was the boyfriend," Tommy remembered. "The military police probably contacted me and they brought me right into the police station and gave me the third degree. I knew almost all of the cops in Maplewood because I would go to town over the summers.

"Once the police interviewed me, they realized that I could not have done it. But for a while they wanted to find out if I'm the culprit or not. It was very frightening at that time. You are being suspected, you are dating someone and she got strangled to death."

Tommy said the questioning went far beyond his own connections, asking about who she might have known and any possible link to a potential killer: "They really seemed like they had to get all the details on who she hung with. Did she have any enemies?"

Friends said that police brought many of Carol's classmates together in the next few days and would continue to question them in groups because they were coming up blank in terms of clues or suspects. "We were all called in by the police to someone's house and they asked us a lot of questions. I remember one of the police said, 'well it could even be one of you,'" Jane Tishman remembers.

One *Star-Ledger* story that weekend described friends and acquaintances who "filed quietly into Maplewood police headquarters for interrogation" related to the killing. But it said police had "absolutely nothing new" on the investigation.

By Saturday, November 5, papers from New York to Philadelphia splashed Carol's image across front pages and offered lengthy reports.

The Star-Ledger made it Page One news, with a headline that described the hunt for a killer as "pressing" and followed with a lengthier report on Sunday. It said police were baffled that the murder took place so quickly, noting that less than an hour passed between the time Carol was last seen and when her body was found.

"The confusing part of this case is the rapidity of events," Maplewood Police Chief William C. Peto told the press. "We just don't understand how the murderer was able to do such damage in a short time."

The Herald-News of Passaic placed the story in the middle of Page One surrounded by news of an early morning crash that killed two teens, a Paterson mayoral fight, the latest Vietnam battles, flooding in Italy, and President Johnson's prediction of a tax increase.

The Philadelphia Daily News, meanwhile, published a story the same day that described the assailant as a "panic-stricken killer," likely due to his quick work and apparent failed effort to sexually assault Carol. It theorized he stopped in mid-attack either due to an accidental killing or being interrupted and wanting to kill her to avoid being identified later.

N.J. Hunts 'More Than One' In Girl's Killing; Quiz Many

Carol Ann Farino—strangled by unknown assailant.

The New York *Daily News* gave the murder major play—considering it was an out-of-town story—with a detail-rich report that said police believed more than one killer may have been involved. It also reported for the first time that one of Carol's co-workers, Gail Gawlick, recalled a man who had approached Carol as the two walked home from school the previous Monday.

Gail told the paper that the mustached man in his 20's had tried to "...persuade Carol Ann to get into his car, a late-model blue Chevrolet." But she declined, telling him to "get lost," Gail said in the story. She also revealed that the man said to Carol: "Okay, I'll catch up to you some other time."

As each day passed, the police grew more and more frustrated, knowing that as time went on the chances of catching or even naming a suspect grew less and less likely.

Later news reports that week confirmed that her killer probably tried to sexually assault Carol but did not get to finish the effort when she was killed, lending some credence to the theory that it may have been an accident. Her autopsy would later confirm no evidence of sexual attack.

The first *News-Record* story that ran a week after her death, on Nov. 10, 1966, said police had been searching sewers, lots, parks, and other areas for clues, and for Carol's shoes and purse, which were missing when she was found. It also reported the first of what would be several ongoing reward funds for anyone who could help solve the case.

Chief Peto, meanwhile, told the paper that more than 50 people had been questioned in the probe and that the department would press the investigation "if it takes a year."

The next few days after the murder were a whirlwind for Cynthia Farino. The 11-year-old had been blindsided by the brutal murder of her only sister, then thrown into a chaotic aftermath of distraught relatives, probing police, and friends and classmates feeling awkward around her.

She was summoned to the police station just days after the killing and without her parents. The cops apparently wanted her without any influence or parental interference, so she asked her older cousin, Emily, to take her.

"She did not want me going by myself," Cynthia recalled about her cousin, the daughter of Ann's brother. "I sat there for three hours and it was a long, long interview. I had to tell them about all of her boyfriends in Newark. All of her friends, what was she interested in? All kinds of stuff. They were shocked that I knew so much about Carol, maybe because of my age."

Cynthia said it was very probing, down to Carol's sexual proclivities and personal actions, and was allegedly tape recorded. "Then I never heard from them again," she said of the police. They later told her they lost the recording.

That began a long dispute among Cynthia, her parents, and the Maplewood Police over how the case was handled. "They were inept at what they were doing, they had no idea what they were doing," Cynthia contends. "I have nothing good to say about the Maplewood Police Department or the prosecutors for that matter at that time."

(More on that later)

After the police were done with Cynthia, her parents did not seem to know how to handle her as they made funeral plans and reached out to relatives. The entire weekend was spent with guests coming to town, some staying at the Jefferson Avenue house and others offering help and support.

Ann and Frank's decision for Cynthia was not to keep her safe and protected at home, but to place her with a family she hardly knew.

"I don't know how that came about. My parents kind of palmed me off because they didn't want me to see and hear everything," Cynthia said years later. "I guess they just volunteered to help because I didn't know them. That was my first year of junior high. We didn't go to the same school."

That family was The Musums, fellow parishioners of Our Lady of Sorrows Church in South Orange, but not close friends. The family, who had two daughters and a son, had offered to take Cynthia in for at least a day or two—a strange but not entirely unusual move in those days when families were struck with tragedy.

Anita Musum, the oldest child, was in Cynthia's grade but attended Our Lady of Sorrows School. She recalls her as a well-mannered but quiet visitor during that strange time.

"I remember that it was a very quiet time, we barely spoke," Anita, who still lives in Maplewood, said about the odd situation. "I remember her father bringing her to my house. I didn't know she was coming. My father took me aside and told me that Cindy would stay with us for a few days. It came out of nowhere. It was just mind-blowing that this person had been murdered. I had only met Carol maybe once. We were friendly but we were like park friends."

Anita, also 10 or 11 at the time, said she heard about the brutal murder of Carol at the same time she learned of this surprise guest from her father. "When he told me her sister had been murdered it scared me to death," said Anita, herself a mother of three today. "It was unheard of that anybody would be murdered. Then to have her sister be in my house."

Anita described Cynthia as polite, but quiet. They shared her bedroom for one or two nights and briefly became friends.

"We sat on the bed in my room and we may have snuck a cigarette. We had two beds, so my sister slept in one bed and Cindy and I slept together in the other," Anita recalled. "It was the kind of a thing where she came down to dinner and was pretty quiet."

Anita also took her temporary roommate to school at least one of the days after the killings. But since it was not Cynthia's regular school—and a private Catholic institution at that—she felt very out of place, even though the teacher was welcoming.

"My father had asked if she could go to school with me. The principal at Our Lady of Sorrows allowed her to come in," Anita said. "She was with the kids in our class and she didn't have a uniform or anything, but she was really in shock as far as I remember. She stayed with us that very first night. She must have stayed with us through the weekend."

Like many Maplewood residents, the killing left a sharp impression on families, especially those with young daughters like the Musums.

"I got a good lecture from my father about never getting in a stranger's car," Anita said. "My daughters would be the first to tell you that I was extremely overprotective of them. I always had to know where they were. They would joke that I was always driving around asking people who had seen them."

Cynthia remembers feeling awkward in a different school with people she did not know and all the time trying to process what had just happened to her sister and her family.

"I was seated in the back of the classroom and the nun was nice and young, she said 'we got a little peanut in the back of the classroom,'" Cynthia remembers. "They were very nice to me. I felt funny, why am I here? I remember feeling very strange."

Cynthia returned to her regular school about 10 days after the murder and felt an awkwardness that would continue for years until she herself graduated from Columbia High School: "I went back to school fairly quickly. About a week after, the Monday after. My teachers didn't know how to act. That was strange."

But those first few days following Carol's death continued to be a wave of uncertainty for Ann and Frank Farino as they grew more protective of their only remaining daughter, but unsure how to comfort her.

Frank would go out on his own on occasion trying to find the killer, while Ann withdrew more and more and became distraught for weeks.

"He was running around town asking stupid questions, trying to find out who did it himself," Cynthia said about her father. "One night my mother was so out of it that she passed out at the dinner table and they had to take her upstairs."

The Galante Funeral Home sat smack in the middle of Vailsburg, the Newark neighborhood where Carol Farino took her first steps as a young child living just blocks away. The family-owned morgue along Sanford Avenue was a mainstay of the community, handling most of the arrangements for the local families, many of whom still remembered when the Farinos lived nearby.

Most of their customers were the usual loved ones who'd lost a family member, either from aging or disease, or perhaps a tragic car accident or fire. A 17-year-old girl brutally murdered with her own stocking was an unusual and especially upsetting affair.

So when Galante was called into handle Carol's wake and burial, staffers knew they had to proceed delicately and with sensitivity. They also braced for what would likely be a large crowd of friends, relatives, and sympathetic mourners from both their neighborhood and Carol's more recent home, Maplewood.

Her wake went on for two days, a common occurrence at the time, with visitations on Saturday, Nov. 5, and Sunday, Nov. 6, from 2 p.m. to 5 p.m. and 7 p.m. to 10 p.m. It all took place less than 48 hours after her death and 24 hours following her autopsy.

Her parents placed her in a formal white dress that wrapped her lifeless body inside the open coffin that sat in Galante's cozy parlor room. For two days as friends and relatives streamed in, the mood was more somber than most wakes, more helpless than if she had died some other way, and more angry that her killer remained on the loose.

"I'll never get over that open casket, I'll never forget that," said classmate Bill Eisner. "They tried to cover up the bruises on her neck, but it was visible. It was the end of youth when you see stuff like that."

The guests ranged from classmates and new Maplewood friends to family members and acquaintances from just around the block. The guest book carried Longfellow's "The Reaper and the Flowers", which stated, in part:

There is a reaper whose name is death.
And, with his sickle keen.
He reaps the bearded grain at a breath.
And the flowers that grow between.

One group of guests at the wake that stood out clearly were the police officers and detectives. A common element of police work in these cases is to see if the killer shows up to see his victim put to rest.

One person who was not there was Cynthia Farino. She said her parents kept her away to protect her, but she felt more neglected than protected.

"The wake was a mob scene, I heard, and cops were there checking out the crowd, undercover detectives there to see what was happening," she said. "I didn't go to the cemetery either, nobody knew what to do with me."

But when Carol's memorial service took place that Monday at 10 a.m., Cynthia was among the swarm of guests who attended at Our Lady of Sorrows Church in South Orange.

The guest registry boasted hundreds of names, including one Robert Kisch, who for some reason wrote in the book that he was senior class president.

"I remember that my mother wanted me to wear a coat I didn't want to wear, I did it because it pleased her," Cynthia remembered. "I remember walking in the church and I didn't want to move, I was stunned. Then someone pushed me from behind into a pew. I was at a standstill and I guess I was holding everyone up."

She described the church as "packed to the rafters. There were reporters, cops, the family and friends, and some of her teachers. It was just insane."

Ann Farino was so overcome that she had to be helped down the aisle to the family's first-row pew: "They had to have two people walk my mother down the aisle because she was in such bad shape. I think she was on sedatives. They had to make sure she was able to walk that far."

Cynthia recalled feeling on display, as though everyone was watching her and the family, perhaps more than at most funerals because of the criminal circumstances.

"I was shocked and I didn't want to be there because I knew I was being watched for a reaction," she explained. "I don't like being on display, I hate all of that stuff. I was numb, I was very shut down and it felt like survival mode." That was a feeling that would follow the younger sibling for much of the rest of her life, she said.

"After it was over I walked outside and was sitting on the side and I saw Tommy [Solomine] walk outside and he started to cry, I never saw a man cry like that."

Cynthia was also not allowed to go to the burial at Gate of Heaven Cemetery in Hanover. "They kind of left me there and I guess I went

back to Anita's house. The first time I saw my sister's grave was when my mother died [in 2015] and we took her there."

Ann and Frank seemed to withdraw as parents in many ways after Carol's death as far as compassion and comfort were concerned, a situation Cynthia said affects her to this day.

"I should have had a therapist after she died, I should have had a tutor to help with my grades, but they didn't do anything to help me after," she said.

In many ways, the wake, funeral, and burial were able to put a degree of closure on Carol's murder. But as the police investigation continued, it only opened more wounds, many of which still exist today.

While Carol Ann Farino was able to rest in peace, Frank, Ann, and especially Cynthia would spend the rest of their lives looking for peace of their own as her killer remained on the loose.

Chapter Four

Frank and Ann Farino first met in late 1939 in the Ironbound section of Newark, N.J., in an area known as Down Neck. Both were natives of New Jersey's largest city and the children of Italian immigrants.

Frank, born in 1918, was one of four sons of Anthony Farino and Clara Brovaco. Ann, a year younger, was the youngest of Vincent and Mary Luciani's nine children.

Ironbound, named for its proximity to Newark Penn Station, was a strong Portuguese and Italian area. Down Neck got its moniker because it was close to a bend in the Rahway River.

Dating back to the 1830s, the area became known for tanning, brewing, and dye production. In the early 20th century, Portuguese and Spanish first arrived, along with African-Americans.

It was at Ann's sister Emma's wedding to Frank's cousin, Sidney Brovaco, where the future parents of Carol and Cynthia first laid eyes on each other. It's not known if they danced.

What is known is that Ann had her eye on another man at the time, a semi-boyfriend whom she'd known since high school. Barely 20 years old at the time, Ann had hoped her beau would pop the question, but instead he went off to college and lost touch.

When Frank appeared—a strong, young, and friendly local product—Ann was swept up, but always with a torch for her previous love. Some thought Frank actually got her on the rebound, as she would always seem somewhat disappointed and even depressed at times.

Ann had been forced to drop out of high school years earlier as the Great Depression hit her family hard, and Frank's as well. Cynthia recalls her mother mentioning she barely had one quality dress to wear to school.

"She had to quit high school because she didn't have enough clothes to wear, she had one skirt and one scarf and that was not enough to wear," Cynthia recalls. "I think she envied my sister and me, that we went much further than her, she was jealous of that."

Frank's family wasn't much better off as the rising unemployment rate struck the Ironbound as much as anywhere, Cynthia explained: "He said they ate potatoes day and night and he had jobs all the time, his parents were very poor."

Newark had come through a positive time for New Jersey in the 1920s. Newark Airport opened in 1928 and other Garden State entities thrived, such as Bell Laboratories and the Camden-Philadelphia Bridge construction. Wright Aeronautical Company launched in Paterson, "placing the Garden State at the fore of the emerging age of commercial aviation," according to *A Time for Despair, A Time for Hope: New Jersey in the Great Depression* by Arthur Guarino, a Rutgers University professor.

Prohibition also brought some of the first illegal and mob activity to the city in the early 1920s, with popular Police Commissioner William Brennan, known for his pro-bootlegger policies.

"The commissioner thought Prohibition a foolish, prudish restriction on liberty," author Brad R. Tuttle wrote in his book, *How Newark Became Newark*. "He took rudimentary steps to follow the law, but frequently argued matters were largely out of his hands."

But when the stock market crashed in 1929, the reverberations did not take long to travel across the Hudson River.

"When the Great Depression hit, thousands of New Jerseyans who lost jobs began to rely on relief funds to feed their families," Guarino wrote. "Teachers, firemen, policemen, and city workers were denied pay raises when the economies of their cities started to go bad. Sometimes, these same towns and cities could not afford to pay anything at all: if you were a teacher or policeman in New Jersey during the Great Depression you often worked for nothing."

Being Italian immigrants, the Lucianis and Farinos were doubly struck, as any jobs went to locals with more American roots. Competition increased as the city's population was growing and would hit 429,000 by 1940, about 50% higher than it would be 60 years later.

Guarino said that New York was the epicenter of the Great Depression with Wall Street and other finance and manufacturing centers. But that led to a ripple effect for the rest of New York City and the metropolitan area.

"New Jersey really depended upon New York City economy and a lot of the manufacturing was sold to New Yorkers and they had no one to sell products to," he said in an interview. "You had a substantial number of clothing manufacturers in New Jersey. It was easy to do and labor was very cheap. Everything made here was sold here, in Newark, and Paterson had tons of factories."

Paterson was known as Silk City. Newark had major department stores such as Hahne's and Quackenbush that employed thousands, many of them immigrants. Newark was also home to several breweries— Budweiser, Rheingold, and Pabst.

"The workers, mainly an immigrant workforce, were cheap, but they were skilled, 99% of them came over from Europe and worked for cheap wages," Guarino said. So when those jobs went with the economic crisis, the workers hit bottom.

In 1938, a year before Ann and Frank met, 16,775 Newark workers were on welfare. Their families muddled through with whatever manual labor was available.

Ann's father, Vincent, ran a local tavern that also served as a speakeasy during prohibition. Frank's father, Anthony, worked in a number of jobs and the fellow Italian neighbors helped each other survive.

"Practically everyone who was Italian lived there and they all knew each other," Cynthia recalled.

Ann and Frank were married only a short time before he joined the U.S. Army, with eyes on the Army Air Corps, the precursor to today's U.S. Air Force. He signed up for duty the day after the Dec. 7, 1941, Pearl Harbor attack, along with tens of thousands of other Americans.

At first, Frank was stationed in Biloxi, Mississippi, and later Charleston, S.C., before being shipped to the Philippines. Ann would travel to both U.S. locations and stay for weeks at a time in rented rooms at local homes, Cynthia said.

Ann and Frank Farino
on their wedding day

"He didn't want to have children, my mother told me that once," she recalled. "He never talked about the Philippines when he was still in the Army Air Corp there. He eventually washed out and had to serve the rest of his time in the Army."

Frank Farino during
World War II

Cynthia remembers one overseas tale of the military when Frank accidentally set his tent on fire: "He burned everything he owned and they had to give him a POW jumpsuit to wear until they got him situated."

After the war, Ann and Frank moved west within Newark, close to Vailsburg, a more suburban neighborhood on Newark's western tip, not far from Maplewood and South Orange and a world away from the Ironbound.

Their first home was at 490 S. 12th Street, near the West Side Park, in a small house that's now replaced by a low-key auto repair business. They later moved further west to Boylan Street, which separated even more from the rest of Newark when the Garden State Parkway opened in 1955, sharply dividing the city both geographically and economically.

"It was a close-knit neighborhood, safe, everyone looked out for everyone and felt safe," Scott Deitche, author of *Garden State Gangland*, said about Vailsburg. "It was a stepping-stone for people who grew up in Newark, it was the next step up."

Filmmaker Marylou Bongiorno, producer of *Revolution '67*, about Newark's historic changes and other related documentaries, echoed Deitche's view.

"The community centered around the church often. People owned their own homes," she said about Vailsburg. "They were very strong communities. Communities that were very much watching out for each other. It was one of these enclaves. Once you get off that Parkway exit, you ask if it is still part of Newark."

Ann and Frank lived and worked in and near Vailsburg, with both of their families still across town in The Ironbound for the most part. Once the war ended, the area grew even more familial and friendly as more inner-city residents relocated to the western neighborhoods.

*Ann and Frank Farino
as newlyweds*

"Vailsburg, North Newark, Weequahic had similar neighborhoods, these were immigrant enclaves. It was a common thing for immigrant groups who gathered and were in the process of making it to come in," said Dr. Thomas A. McCabe, a board member of the Newark History Society and a history professor at Rutgers University, Newark. "Irish, Italian, Romanian all moved to Vailsburg. It was kind of a second stop on that American journey. The final stop was the move out of the city."

Vailsburg had about 35,000 people at the time. Mostly immigrants and few people of color, he said.

"A large town, a small city in its own right. One of the defining features of Vailsburg was the coming of the Garden State Parkway. It kind of insulates the neighborhood, creates this kind of otherness, its own suburb," McCabe said. "It had a great park there, Vailsburg Park, ball playing, bike riding, and good schools. It had its own high school, a massive Catholic parochial school, Sacred Heart. You had thousands of people going to mass there on Sunday."

The Farinos worked and saved for several years in the area as Ann took jobs, including one at a photography studio, and Frank drove a truck, among other professions that included clerking at Weber & Co. Hardware in north Newark. Life was tough but often positive.

Ten years of marriage passed as they survived war, money troubles, and family squabbles before the biggest change occurred: parenthood! A change that would later bring the biggest challenge in their lives.

Carol Ann Farino was born at 6:39 a.m. on July 9, 1949, at East Orange General Hospital. She weighed in at a healthy 7 pounds, 2 ounces, and stretched out at 19 and a half inches.

The big news elsewhere in the world, according to that day's *New York Times* front page, included a mistrial in the Alger Hiss case, an update on the British dock strike, congressional approval of a low-income housing plan, and a raise for federal cabinet secretaries along with more than 20 government officials.

Carol Ann Farino

But all eyes in the Farino and Luciani families were on their newest member, who drew a continuous flow of relatives to Ann Farino's hospital room.

The hospital was seven blocks from the Farinos' home at 78 Boylan St. at the time, a three-story apartment building. They would later move three homes down to 84 Boylan, the first floor of a two-family house, after Cynthia joined the brood five years later.

Through the next seven years the family of four made Boylan Street their home as the girls attended nearby Alexander Street School, Frank and Ann became part of the local social groups and worked nearby, and the neighborhood flourished as one of Newark's most desirable areas.

"It was wonderful, everyone would sit out on the porches and we'd play kick the can and hide-and-seek," Cynthia recalls about those early days. "It was a lot more fun than Maplewood, it was a community. It was a whole different ballgame.

"It was basically a middle-class kind of place, it was Irish in the 40s and a lot of Italians moved up from the 14th ward," she said. "I walked everywhere. We would walk from Vailsburg to West Side Park and back. Everybody knew everybody. We walked at night."

But that's when the cracks started to deepen in the Farinos' marriage, according to Cynthia. Frank's temper

Ann, Frank, Cynthia & Carol Farino

would flare up when money issues arose or his over-protective personality roared to life. With two daughters in what was still a big city, even if the neighborhood was deemed safe, Frank dealt with stresses every day, or at least perceived stresses.

He knew boys were on the prowl as in every town, but his view took it more seriously and often with overreaction.

The Farino family

"When we lived in Newark, we lived in a two-family house and our landlady lived upstairs," Cynthia explained. "She would later tell the cops how he would holler and scream all the time."

She said it was a tight-knit community where families watched over each other and parents would keep an eye on each other's offspring.

"Everybody was Italian on our street, that was great, everybody understood everybody, we had the same culture and background," Cynthia recalled.

As the years passed, more Italians and other immigrant families would move in and keep the area safe. The religious ties were strong, as were the working-class connections among most of the residents.

"Because it was so far from downtown Newark, it had come to be seen as a real refuge for a lot of the middle-class whites in the '50s and '60s," Steven Elliott, a Rutgers Newark history professor said about Vailsburg. "For a while, it held on to that more middle- and upper-middle-class white identity, compared to the central ward that was becoming overwhelmingly Black."

Vailsburg was a separate entity for years, joining as the last piece of Newark in 1904. A *New York Times* report on that 100-year anniversary in 2004 describes the neighborhood's prominence in power and legal authority over the years.

"What Weequahic was to the Jews of [author Philip] Roth's generation, Vailsburg was to a mixture of Irish, Italian, German, and Ukrainian immigrants and their children," the story stated. "Many of them had fled other parts of the city—the Irish from Down Neck, the Italians from the 14th Ward. The breadwinners were police and firemen, operating engineers, brewery workers, Board of Education employees and, in the brick homes along Eastern Parkway, doctors, lawyers, and dentists."

That was the Farinos to a tee.

"Vailsburg was also home to Newark's governing elite, beginning with a prominent lawyer who went on to become a Supreme Court Justice, William Brennan, the son of an Irish immigrant and labor union organizer." the *Times* added. "Mayors like Vince Murphy and Leo Carlin and Hugh Addonizio lived in Vailsburg, along with countless members of the City Council and chairmen of the Essex County Democratic Party. Two future Democratic state chairmen, Ray Durkin and Thomas Giblin, grew up within shouting distance of each other."

It also pointed out the church community, mentioning that many were parishioners at Sacred Heart Roman Catholic Church on South Orange Avenue. "That church was the focus of life in Vailsburg," State Supreme Court Justice James Zazzali, a Rumson resident who was born in the neighborhood in 1937 and lived there until his marriage in 1967, told the *Times*. "It was a classic immigrant church and was the largest church in the city at the time."

The report also described Vailsburg as "[t]he political capital of Newark, its influence felt in Newark City Hall as well as the State House in Trenton."

"It was very much a political culture," added Brendan O'Flaherty of Columbia University who lived in Vailsburg from 1958 to 1994. "It was the political hub of the city."

And then there was the mob.

Organized crime in New Jersey has a long and storied history, and more recent fame with the success of *The Sopranos*. While that HBO hit is fiction, it's based on many real cases and a clear pattern of abuse and power struggles dating back more than 100 years.

Mix it with New Jersey's political history of corruption that has often crossed the line with gangster elements, and the impact in such an older and densely populated state is not surprising.

"The state's reputation as a hotbed of organized crime is one that is not entirely undeserved," veteran Newark Star-Ledger reporter Robert Rudolph wrote in his 1992 book, *The Boys From New Jersey*. "After all, how many other states can boast the distinction of having had an entire police department indicted and suspended for accepting gifts from a Mafia chieftain?"

Rudolph was referring to the 1969 indictments of five members of the tiny Old Tappan Police Department in Bergen County who were accused of being paid off by mob boss Vinny "The Chin" Gigante in exchange for informing him of surveillance on his home.

But the state's organized criminal history dates back further than that to one Albert Anastasia, the leader of the so-called Murder Incorporated enterprise. After making his mark in the 1920s and 1930s with the longshoremen's unions of Brooklyn—including operations ranging from loan sharking to murder for hire—Anastasia relocated to Fort Lee, New Jersey, in 1940, where he lived until his murder in 1957.

There was also Prohibition-era bootlegger Arthur Flagenheimer, known more commonly as "Dutch Schultz." He gained fame in 1935 for putting a contract out on then-Manhattan District Attorney and future Republican Presidential candidate Thomas E. Dewey.

But when fellow mobsters found out about the plan, they objected, fearing it would spark an even harsher crackdown on their operations. After Schultz refused to back off, he was shot to death in the Palace Chop House in Newark, just blocks from the Ironbound.

I saw much of the mob's New Jersey influence during my first reporting job at the former *Daily Journal* in Elizabeth. Between 1988 and 1990 I covered some of the major cities of Union County, which borders Newark's Essex County.

Those included Union, Linden, and Elizabeth—all with ties to mob boss John Riggi, who headed the New Jersey-based DeCavalcante crime family in the 1980s. A graduate of Linden High School and a World War II U.S. Army Air Corps veteran, Riggi eventually controlled many labor unions and demanded payoffs to avoid labor strikes, created no-show jobs, and oversaw loan-sharking and gambling, among other things.

Riggi pleaded guilty to extortion in 1992 and was sentenced to 12 years in prison. In 1990, the FBI set up surveillance with wiretaps at the former Daphne's Restaurant in the Newark Airport Sheraton, where Riggi would often meet with associates. The move proved successful by collecting evidence that helped put him away.

Rumors spread for years that Riggi was the inspiration for Tony Soprano's character, given creator David Chase's New Jersey roots. But after Riggi died in 2015, Chase revealed that the fictional mob boss was based on Richie Boiardo, a one-time milkman who turned bootlegger in the 1930s. Known as "Richie The Boot," he lived in the same neighborhood as Chase's mother, Newark's First Ward on the city's north side.

By the time the Farinos settled in Vailsburg in the 1950s, Newark's organized crime presence had spread there as well... not in the sense that it saw violent gangland hits or local business payoff demands, but as a place for many crime bosses and their families to call home.

"Vailsburg was definitely a well-known mobbed-up neighborhood, it was pretty Italian. And the area between Vailsburg and downtown Newark, there was a lot of mob activity there," author Scott Dietche said. "Illegal gambling was big in that area and they also ran casinos in the Ironbound, underground casinos and card games, dice games. I would not be surprised if they got into narcotics."

Vailsburg was where the crime bosses and crew members often lived and a place they kept safe with efforts to kick out any problematic interlopers.

Chief among the Farinos' neighbors there were the Campisi Family, which had reputed ties to several crime organizations, including the Genovese crime family.

Led by Peter A. Campisi, family members engaged in various criminal enterprises and operated along South Orange Avenue in the 1950s and 1960s, just blocks from the Farinos' Vailsburg home.

"An Essex County law enforcement official said the Campisis were used as enforcers and 'hit men' by the Mafia but generally were considered 'too whacked out' and unreliable to be given full Mafia family membership," *The New York Times* reported in a lengthy 1973 story about indictments of 10 family members and associates.

"The six-count state indictment was hailed by law-enforcement officials here as the 'most complete picture' ever presented of underworld activities because, for the first time, the violence was shown to support a gambling and narcotics empire. The targets of the indictment are eight members of the Campisi family, all blood relatives, and two other members of their gang."

The charges claimed that the family "conspired to control, supervise and operate dice games, horse betting and the numbers lottery" in six counties. It added that proceeds from armed robberies funded gambling operations and the family allegedly used bribery and threats of violence to influence jurors and witnesses in legal proceedings.

Several murder victims were described as "disloyal associates in gambling and narcotics enterprises," suspected police informants, and potential prosecution witnesses, *The Times* stated, adding they were also charged with plotting to kill three other crime rivals, but the killings never occurred.

In one case, Campisi members took "meticulous care to details," the indictment said. One murder victim was allegedly sprinkled with pepper so that stray dogs would not dig up his grave.

"They were a family that was not quite mob," O'Flaherty of Columbia recalls. "That area was mob, Alexander Street School was mob. I went to school with these guys, their kids, and cousins. They hung out at the Roundtable on South Orange Avenue."

That would be The Roundtable Lounge, which the Campisis owned and was known as a top meeting place for many of their criminal operations. They also ran the Cabaret Lounge about a half-mile away. Peter R. Campisi owned it with his sister, Connie.

"The Roundtable was once a favorite hangout for the state's most no-

8

torious and underworld figures," The *Asbury Park Press* wrote in a 1976 story about the family's later dealings. "It prospered until the Campisi empire started to go downhill." The lounge was sold after the 1973 indictments.

Connie also operated a beauty salon in the area, which served many of the Campisi Family's wives and girlfriends, according to Anita Musum, the Maplewood neighbor with whom Cynthia stayed briefly after Carol's death.

Anita's father, John, ran a major beauty supply company in Newark at the time and strictly prohibited her from going near the salon.

"I once told him how I wanted to go there," she said. "He said if I ever catch you in there you'll regret it."

The family's time in Newark dated back to 1916 when patriarch Pietro Campisi emigrated from Italy, the *Press* wrote. He and his wife had seven sons, many of whom worked small-time criminal operations in Vailsburg, including a numbers racket that investigators claimed ran into the thousands, often with police help in many cases.

Some 16 indictments and dozens of arrests of family members would occur between 1964 and 1972, but most were dismissed for a variety of reasons. They included gambling, weapons, and assault.

Bob Buccino, author of *New Jersey Mob: Memoirs of a Top Cop* and a former state law enforcement officer, described them as "a violent renegade group" that "committed every crime imaginable. They ran gambling houses, sold drugs, and committed armed robberies. You name it and they did it."

The family finally saw a real dent in its operations in the 1970s when the federal indictments led to guilty pleas by nine family members and associates who were sentenced to terms ranging from three to 75 years. Much of the evidence rested on former Campisi associate Ira Pecznick, who had agreed to testify against many of his former partners in exchange for a lighter sentence for an armed robbery conviction.

Information about the family is oddly difficult to find. Two books have been written about them but are out of print, and rare copies have become a costly investment.

One account, titled *To Drop A Dime*, was written in 1976 by Pecznick and writer Paul Hoffman. But you won't find it in any local library, while online copies run more than $800.

The only New Jersey library that seemed to have a copy was in Nutley, which kept it only as a reference option. Local crime observers allege that Campisi family members have taken to buying up copies and removing those that had existed for sale.

Another book, *Deal*, by journalist Harvey Aronson, came out in 1978. It's also out of print, priced high online, and missing from area libraries. Aronson, now 93, did not respond to requests to discuss the Campisis.

Cynthia said the crime family did not disrupt the neighborhood but was a clear presence in local shops and eateries and straight out of a Hollywood film or The Sopranos in some ways.

"They were all over the place. There was a bar around the corner, a lounge, on the block after my street, they used to hang out outside, all the big guys. Like *Goodfellas*," she said. "I used to see them when I would go for lemon ice. They kept things safe, we could play games in the street until midnight. The parents would be sitting on the porches and my mother never worried about us being outside."

Frank Farino was even approached once with an offer of underworld help following Carol's murder years later but declined. "I thought that was really stupid because the police weren't doing anything so why not take their help?" Cynthia said.

She claims her family was never involved in the illegal mob activities. "My father was a truck driver. If we were in the mob we would have lived a lot better than we did."

So when The Farinos decided to move out of Newark it was not the mob's influence as much as Newark's growing civil rights battles and increased white flight that began in the late 1950s and early 1960s.

"There was white flight," said filmmaker Bongiorno. "From the 1950s on you were seeing this migration to the suburbs. You are also talking about bank redlining, federal policies that made it easier to move to the suburbs, but not for the African-American community."

Historian McCabe agreed: "There was the rising African-American population. By the 1950s Newark becomes a majority black population, the central ward, and the downtown. African-Americans started moving in more and you got a steady increase."

Cynthia said it was not so much a racist view on her parents' part that prompted the move to Maplewood at the time, but more fears of related protests and even riots. Although the famed 1967 Newark Uprising would not occur for several years, the neighborhood was changing.

"The only problem we ever had was when they had a riot at the public pool, a real riot at the pool," Cynthia said. "That's when my father started thinking we needed to get out of there. We also moved to Maplewood because our

Carol Ann Farino

doctor was in Maplewood and I had asthma and they wanted to live in Maplewood because they had gotten to know it as a nice place."

In 1964 the family left Boylan Street behind for a new life on Jefferson Avenue in Maplewood. Safer streets, a nicer house, and better schools. And, of course, one unforgettable night.

But the Newark connection would come back to haunt them, especially Frank Farino. When the police begin to investigate the tragedy of Carol Ann Farino, Vailsburg's criminal ties would be drawn in as investigators seized upon her father in a way that may well have taken them off course and led to the unsolved status of the case today.

Chapter Five

William C. Peto had been with the Maplewood Police for more than 20 years when Carol Ann Farino was killed, but he had only been chief of police for two years.

In those two years, however, the township had already seen at least one tragic murder. The same year that Peto was appointed chief, a 38-year-old bus driver, Elwood Hadley, had walked unannounced into the Maplewood home of his wife's parents and shot her in the head.

The day before, Hadley's wife, Madeline, 33, had walked out on him with their two children, ages one and four, and left their Woodbridge, N.J., home after an argument. Press accounts said he approached the parents' Maplewood home on quiet, tree-lined Bowdoin Street in broad daylight on March 19, 1964.

Madeline was in the kitchen where Elwood entered and shot her once in the head with a .38 caliber revolver, then turned the gun on himself. He died eight days later in a local hospital. Police later found a live hand grenade and a .45 caliber handgun in his car.

When police eventually searched their Woodbridge home, they called in U.S. Army demolition experts, believing Hadley may have boo-by-trapped the residence. Although investigators found three cans of gunpowder and several detonation devices, no set explosives were discovered.

Oddly, just three years earlier, Hadley had made out a new will that left his entire estate to Madeline, even though he had two teenaged children from a previous marriage.

Peto had seen other strange murder cases in town. One year after joining the police force in 1947, there was the case of Frederick S. Dieter of Meadowbrook Place. The 76-year-old retired jeweler "ran amok" in his home, as one news story described it, on a Sunday morning in May of that year.

Later claiming he was worried about the planned construction of dozens of garden apartments next to his home, Dieter shot his son to death and wounded his wife and daughter-in-law before attempting suicide twice during a standoff with police.

After a 20-minute gun battle with cops, Dieter was taken into custody with the use of tear gas and held at a nearby hospital on psychiatric observation.

Dieter, who also shot his dog in the incident, later signed a statement that said he feared the 130-unit apartment complex would force him to fence in his backyard that he had spent years beautifying. A news report said "[H]e was certain his family's privacy and comfort were now at an end and that therefore he didn't want to leave behind anybody he loved."

He was ordered to New Jersey State Hospital at Trenton where he died years later.

Then there was the 1952 shooting of a Newark youth in South Mountain Reservation, allegedly through a murder-for-hire arrangement.

But those were all solved relatively quickly, as the killers knew their victims and were caught red-handed. When Chief Peto was handed the Farino murder he had no clear suspects, no witnesses, and a murder weapon made of stocking material.

A South Orange native, Peto was one of six children born to Louis and Margert Peto. Louis Peto was a longtime South Orange cop who died in 1979.

The younger Peto attended Our Lady of Sorrows School in South Orange, then Seton Hall Preparatory School, and the state police academy in Trenton. He was attending Seton Hall University but left in 1942 to serve in the U.S. Army in Europe. He received the Silver Star and later remained in the Army Reserve until 1963.

Peto became a sergeant in 1959 and a lieutenant in 1962. Much of his time before becoming chief was spent in law enforcement academics as an instructor at the Essex County Police Academy and in other similar pursuits, with less emphasis on detective work or homicide cases. He also served six years as the head of Essex County's Association of Chiefs of Police.

In 1958, while still a detective, Peto was among the founders of Maplewood's Decent Literature Committee, one of many nationwide at the time that sought to pressure local bookstores and newsstands to stop selling material they found offensive. The group lasted only a few years.

"Bill was very nice, very polite, and very gentle. He was very quiet and reserved. I think a lot of people didn't know him well, including his family. He was so quiet about things," said Howard Bendrot, who married one of Peto's five children, his daughter, Patricia. "He took the responsibility of the job and never discussed it. He would never want anyone to hear something on the street that he might have mentioned to the family. He knew what his job was and did not want to jeopardize that."

There was the time when his wife was pulled over for speeding in Maplewood and ticketed. When Peto heard about it, he supported the officer. "That's what you should do," Bendrot recalled him saying to the cop. "Those were the kinds of stories you would hear about him."

Peto was also instrumental in starting the Maplewood First Aid Squad.

"One of the things was that the police in Maplewood used to run their own ambulance. He was chief and it was becoming too much for the police department to handle," Bendrot said. "So he had one of his officers lead the project to start a volunteer first aid squad. We were charter members of that."

But the former chief, who retired in 1976, always had regret for that unsolved murder case, Bendrot said. Although he wouldn't discuss it often, he could never quite get over the one that got away.

"When he talked about his career that was the one thing that he would mention, that they never solved the murder of Carol Farino," Bendrot recalls. "He wasn't happy with that because it was an unsolved crime. He didn't have much to say about it, but he felt bad that it was an unsolved murder in town. I think he was upset because it was a senseless murder."

It's unclear how complete or in-depth the Maplewood Police investigations were, according to Cynthia Farino, Carol's sister. Even decades later, she recalls an investigation she found incomplete and misguided.

"There were a lot of things that were mishandled. I could write out a list," Cynthia said in 2020. "They didn't know what to do."

Maplewood Police and the Essex County Prosecutor's Office were reluctant to provide details of the investigation over the years beyond the initial police reports. Both declined access to police files on the case despite the fact it dated back more than 50 years.

The Essex County Prosecutor's Office sent me a five-page rambling citation of statutes and laws that they claimed protected them from having to provide information after an Open Public Records Act request was sent.

Cynthia recalls being brought in by police just days after the murder and facing Peto and two other officers for several hours of questioning.

"Peto seemed very nervous and he started to get a nosebleed," Cynthia remembers. "He interviewed me with two other cops, they asked me questions for a couple of hours. But they kept me waiting a long time."

Cynthia remembers the interview being tape-recorded but was later told the recording had been lost or destroyed. She said the police had very little contact with the family in the next weeks and months.

"I don't remember them coming over to my house at all," Cynthia said. "I don't think they tried to do much, they tried to sweep it under the rug as much as they could," she added. "It was an embarrassment to Maplewood. That is why I lived out of the state for a while."

News accounts and personal recollections of those involved at the time of the killing paint a mixed picture of the law enforcement effort. Police at the time claimed to have interviewed more than 300 people about the case and said that the Prosecutor's Office had dedicated four investigators to the probe initially.

A story in *The News-Record*, Maplewood and South Orange's weekly newspaper, weeks after Carol's murder quoted a seemingly desperate Chief Peto begging readers for information as the case stalled.

Anyone having "the slightest shred of evidence" was asked to come forward, the paper stated. "Write a personal, anonymous letter to me with some sure mark of identification on the bottom. If it leads to an apprehension and conviction the person who provided the information will be eligible for a reward."

Rewards were offered within weeks of the killing when the police made it clear they had no clues or suspects. *The News-Record* began soliciting donations for a reward with the Maplewood Bank and Trust Company, which reached $1,300 initially and later grew with a $500 donation by the Maplewood Patrolmen's Benevolent Association.

Two other anonymous donations came later that brought it to $2,300 by early 1967. The township added another $3,000 that year to bring it to more than $5,000.

Still, no suspects were found or arrested.

Since Peto's background offered little in the area of breaking a tough murder case like Carol's and the township had few murders at all during its short history at the time, it's not surprising they might have been ill-equipped to handle such a perplexing case.

One unique element of this homicide was the slim timeline involved—a short 60 minutes or less. Since Carol was last seen in Maplewood Village around 7:30 p.m. and her body was found about an hour later just a mile or so away, it was clear the deed had been done quickly.

There was also a fairly direct path Carol likely took as she walked home that night—north on Maplewood Avenue, then east on Jefferson Avenue to her home, less than a mile.

Cynthia said her family was never notified of the specific efforts being made, or even if police had knocked on all doors along Carol's likely path. She recalls no fliers or notices put up around town seeking information.

"It was an embarrassment to Maplewood," she said. "They did not want anyone to know it. Nobody got murdered in Maplewood. It is too bad that they don't want to know this, it happened in their small town."

Carol's death was not the only shocking or notable 1966 murder of a young woman in New Jersey. Prior to her killing, four other women, all under 21, suffered brutal murders that year, each of which remained unsolved for many years.

Joanne Fantazier, 17, of Perth Amboy was abducted on Feb. 10, 1966, struck in the head with a blunt object, and thrown off of a bridge in Colts Neck, Monmouth County, while believed to still be alive, but unconscious.

She was found face down on ice over the Yellow Brook below the Muhlenbrink Road bridge, having been dropped twelve feet with her red dress on and still wearing a fur coat. The cause of death was ruled to be a brain hemorrhage due to blunt force trauma and hypothermia. She was not believed to have been sexually assaulted and her case was still unsolved a year later.

On March 8, 1966, seven-year-old Wendy Sue Wolin of Elizabeth in Union County was stabbed to death with a single knife wound in the middle of a Tuesday afternoon as she waited for her mother to pull the family car up from behind their apartment building.

The perpetrator was wearing a mask or other disguise that covered his face and committed the deadly act in front of other children along Irvington Avenue in the county's largest city.

Youngsters who saw the attack described the killer as a middle-aged white man in his mid-forties, stocky, about 220 pounds, with thick grey hair. He was seen walking calmly to nearby Prince Street and dropping a hunting knife about 200 feet away from the scene.

An artist's sketch circulated at the time of an older man in his 40s or 50s with a trench coat and fedora, more an average businessman than a cold-blooded killer.

That horrendous killing of an innocent child went unsolved for decades and would involve more than 300 law enforcement officers over the years, along with some 1,500 interviews. Cops even interviewed troops aboard a Vietnam-bound ship in dock at the Port of Elizabeth at the time.

The case was reopened 29 years later, in 1995, as the Union County Prosecutor's Office believed they had a suspect, but the accusation could never be proven. In 2016, on the 50th anniversary, one Elizabeth police captain started an online campaign to reopen the case, but to no avail. The victim's sister, Jodi, keeps a Facebook page up in her honor.

Catherine Baker, 16, of Edison Township in Middlesex County, was abducted near her home on St. Patrick's Day 1966 and found two months later in nearby Jackson Township. She was discovered floating in the south branch of the Metedeconk River near Cook's Bridge, Jackson Township. She was nude from the waist down with fatal skull fractures,

Baker had left home at 7 p.m. on March 17, headed to a bakery one block away in the Edison Shopping Center on Woodbridge Avenue, to buy cupcakes for her mother.

The case was never completely solved, but on August 13, 1966, a former boyfriend, 18-year-old Ivan Joseph Rule, committed suicide in his cell when he was detained for questioning. Police later found a letter written by Baker to a friend in which she claimed Rule had threatened to kill her if she dated anyone else.

The closest in similarity to Carol's murder might have been the death of Janet Ipsaro Adams, 18, of Paramus in Bergen County. She was found strangled to death in her apartment on April 4, 1966—two days after her wedding to Brian Adams, 24.

The culprit, who has yet to be found, used one of her husband's neckties to strangle her to death. Police quickly ruled out Adams as a suspect when he provided an alibi of being at work.

Janet was found nude in her second-story garage apartment on the bathroom floor with signs of recent sexual activity, a torn bra, and was next to a half-filled bathtub. She had bruises on the forehead and scratches on her hands. A four-inch pair of scissors had been stabbed into her heart, but investigators say she died of the strangulation first.

Janet's killer has never been found, but police had sought to link her death to Richard Cottingham, 73, known as the "Torso Killer" for a string of dozens of murders of young women between 1967 and 1980.

In prison on a life sentence since the 1980s for several murders, Cottingham confessed in early 2020 to killing three other young women in Bergen County in 1968 and 1969, all by strangulation.

Maplewood Police did later seek to link him to Carol's death, given the similarities in the murder style and weapon, but found no real evidence and did not pursue it.

But the most famous Garden State murder in 1966 occurred on June 17, 1966, at the Lafayette Bar and Grill in Paterson, when two men were shot to death in a robbery. The men, bartender James Oliver and customer Fred Nauyoks, were killed immediately. Another patron, Hazel Tanis, died weeks later at a hospital.

The shooting spree brought heightened interest when one of the suspects turned out to be middleweight boxing contender Ruben "Hurricane" Carter. He was arrested and convicted along with a friend, John Artis, after the two were stopped in a car similar to one seen at the murder location later that night.

In the years that followed, however, a wave of public attention on the case—brought about by Carter's fame and claims of a wrongful conviction based on race—kept the calls for Carter's release going. The issue drew national attention again in 1976 when singer Bob Dylan wrote the song "Hurricane" that slammed the investigation and trial as "a pig circus," noting an all-white jury had convicted the two black men.

Carter was eventually released in 1985. He died in 2014.

Homicide experts point to the 24/24 rule as a key element in pursuing such cases, which states cops must comb all possible clues that account for the victim's actions and whereabouts 24 hours before a murder and 24 hours later.

"Detectives want to know the routine of the victim before the victim's death," writes John J. Militech, author of *Homicide Investigation: An Introduction*. "Twenty-four hours after the homicide, the memories of any victims are still relatively fresh. Furthermore, the perpetrator may still be in the community."

The first step is also to interview anyone who knew Carol, according to Carl Malmquist, a criminal psychologist and author of *Homicide: A Psychiatric Perspective*. "They would have wanted to talk to all of the people she worked with and friends and near friends and family members. Talk to classmates," he said. "Depending on how many hours they want to put in on it. You accumulate the list and talk to them one on one, which does take time."

But that takes skill and experience that Maplewood Police may have lacked at the time due to the township's minimal history of homicides. Just interviewing does not mean much if the right approach is not taken, Malmquist said.

"I have seen some interviews that consist of putting down birthdays and names rather than inquiring about how she spent her time, who she knew. That is the kind of interviewing to do and that takes skill," he explained. "Some cops are not interested in that kind of stuff. But interviewing is a skill, just as a reporter, you have to ask the right questions and know which ones to pursue, particularly back then."

"Police now get more sophisticated and they insist on getting some training in this. Most cops back then were not given the kind of training to know how to interview. That is when you get leads that you are not even thinking about until you have these interviews. That is the benefit of good interviewing, you get leads."

But if police focus too much on people she knew, they can stray from considering a stranger, according to Vernon Geberth, a former New York City police commander of the Bronx Division and the author of several books on murder investigations.

"One of the most difficult things in a homicide is you have to eliminate friends and family, you have to go through a whole review of who they knew, who they were friendly with. We want to find out what was going on in his or her life prior to what was going on. That opens the door to a lot of possibilities."

Geberth said of the process dubbed "victimology," "You end up knowing more about the victim than the victim knew about themselves."

It's clear that Maplewood police interviewed just about anyone who knew Carol at the time or had seen or spent time with her. But did that take the focus off the possibility of a stranger and, of course, give that stranger a chance to distance himself from the crime and the community?

"You lose valuable time when you are investigating friends and family," Geberth said. "You lose time if someone had thought this was a stranger, if the focus could have been on that, the investigation is going to go awry."

Experts also point to Carol's job as a waitress in a nighttime cafe in the township's business area.

Milt's Cup and Saucer was both a regular stop for dozens of daily customers and a likely place for strangers passing through town to visit for a quick bite or cup of coffee. Just a block from the train station, any rail rider who needed to down a quick meal would stop in as well.

The surrounding businesses and small apartments of Maplewood Village could have held the answer. But there is no sign that police did any such door-to-door searches or questioning of neighboring residents or merchants beyond those next to the outside of George's Luncheonette, where Carol was last seen.

Motive is also important. Given that Carol's girdle had been pulled down and her stocking removed, police believe attempted sexual assault of some kind was likely. Further evidence found she was not raped and although her undergarments were not removed, they were described as being in a "loosened condition."

Initial reports also speculated that Carol had two killers, given that she would not likely get into a car with a stranger and a lone perpetrator would have difficulty forcing her in alone, according to family and friends.

"If someone picked her up to drive her home, it was someone she knew," Frank Farino told *The Star-Ledger* in a Nov. 6, 1966, story. "Carol never would have gotten into a car with someone she didn't know."

If she was abducted by someone in a car along Maplewood or Jefferson Avenues, it would have been difficult for a lone person to grab her, hold her tightly so she would not escape, and get her into a vehicle without anyone seeing or hearing the incident.

Both streets have homes side by side and close to the street and sidewalk, so completing such a crime alone would seem to be difficult without being noticed. However, if two perpetrators were involved, one could easily drive the vehicle while the other jumped out, surprised Carol, grabbed her from behind, covered her mouth, and forced her into the car.

"While it is very possible she was murdered during a sexual assault, we are not ruling out other possibilities," Chief Peto told the *Newark Evening News* days after the killing. The same story quoted the Essex County Medical Examiner as saying there was a "strong possibility" of an attempted sexual assault.

But to abduct a teenage girl along a busy street, attempt a sexual assault, strangle her to death and dump her body on a public street—all in less than an hour and without being seen by anyone—seemed almost impossible.

The theory of a random killer that Carol did not know was boosted initially by the testimony of her co-worker, Gail Gawlik, mentioned earlier, who told *The News-Record* a man had approached Carol in a car offering a ride days earlier and said he would "catch up" to her later when she declined.

Two incidents of men approaching and seeking to touch other teen girls in Maplewood in later months also add to the theory that the abduction of Carol was random and involved a stranger or strangers.

"It sounds like an interrupted rape and is that what led him to strangle her? Because she could identify him? Or was that an integral part of a sexual act to begin with?" asked Malmquist. "It is really a guessing game. Your first thought is maybe the person got scared in attempting in the midst of a rape and could not complete it. If she was walking in an isolated area."

Both Malmquist and Geberth pointed to Carol's job as a waitress, a profession that draws a variety of customers and many who eye a young, pretty girl as a potential target.

"Did anyone come in wanting to get acquainted with her, suspicions of anyone where she worked?" Malmquist asked.

Geberth agreed: "The fact that she was a waitress opens the door to a lot of possibilities, a lot of perpetrators see an attractive young waitress, they have all the time in the world to follow her."

He speculates that Carol's job, the hour of the evening she was abducted, and the probability she was grabbed on her way home make a stranger who saw her at the diner more of a possibility.

"It could have been someone who saw her and made the decision to stalk her. In his mind, he was going to get something and it wasn't just taking her panties off," Geberth said. "If the person is stalking and knows which way she was going home, he could be parking and waiting for her. The fact that it wasn't completed makes me believe there was a sudden appearance to the offender. These cases don't happen in a vacuum, I would look for some attempts, some stalking complaint."

Gail Gawlick's claim that a man approached her and Carol just days before offering a ride would indicate she was being followed by someone that week. But the contention by police and Frank Farino that Carol would never get into a car with a stranger appears to have taken cops off that track and kept them on the road of believing the killer was someone she knew.

That's a road that Cynthia Farino and her parents suffered from personally, and one she still believes has kept the crime unsolved.

Chapter Six

In the weeks that followed the murder, Cynthia Farino's world became as dark and difficult as possible. Her 12th birthday came and went just nine days after Carol's death and she spent most of the time in her room.

"I used to stay in my room all the time because it was horrible," she recalled, noting she received no counseling or personal sympathy from relatives. "After a month I was supposed to be over it. Everything was supposed to go back to normal."

But normal was the last thing she experienced. Cynthia recalls each of her mother's five sisters coming to stay for about a week at a time and her parents' rocky marriage crumbling further.

"They didn't have a great marriage to begin with, so all of this exacerbated it, his temper was worse and they zeroed in on me," she said. "I was supposed to fix it for them."

Cynthia was back in school within a week of the killings and began to see a strange reaction from other students, friends, and acquaintances alike.

"It was a horrible experience and I became the girl whose sister was murdered," she said. "I couldn't be anonymous if I tried, and it was horrible for me at that age. People felt awkward around me. I had good friends I grew up with but only two or three I felt comfortable with."

Cynthia had only lived in town for two years and was facing that first year of junior high school as a still-new kid at school, she remembered. Walking through Memorial Park each day toward the junior high school, which still sits just a block from the last place Carol had been seen, Cynthia often wondered if her sister's killer was still around, adding to the tension.

She found the awkwardness of others reflected back on her each day.

"I felt that everybody was whispering about me and I did not want to talk to anyone. I didn't have a lot of friends in that year of junior high. I did not want to go out of my way and be conspicuous. I felt like I was this object to be talked about."

In a small town, Cynthia's actions received increased scrutiny. If anyone found her misbehaving it got back to her parents, who would tighten the screws of discipline more.

"I didn't want people knowing everything I did. Everyone knew who I was and I would get caught," she said, noting small missteps such as smoking or cutting class. "I just wanted to get away, send me away to a private school where no one knows me. And they wouldn't do it."

And her parents were no help. Ann's depression only grew and Frank's anger—a mix of guilt and helplessness—made him even more upset and protective of his only remaining child.

"I never did anything that bad. I would drink with my friends and once in a while grass or pills, but they didn't know about that. Anything I did would be a big deal," Cynthia said. "I felt like I couldn't do anything that normal kids did because my parents would find out about it, everyone knew who I was. If I was smoking a cigarette after school, my father would always find out I was smoking."

She said her parents reacted in a mix of guilt and increased discipline that seemed bizarre to her.

"They were ridiculous about stupid things and they would ignore the important ones," Cynthia said. "They were not worried about me going to school but they wouldn't let me go with my friends."

Frank Farino went back to his news delivery job rather quickly as well, while Ann worked part-time at a local discount store just down the street on Valley. Both seemed to want to hide the pain and the image of their suffering family but kept a tight leash on Cynthia.

"They didn't like all of the attention, they were treating it as an embarrassment," she said. "I had never been able to do anything like joining a club or a team, I had to be home right after school. I was such a shy person that I would never join anything, I did not want to be the center of attention."

But inside, Cynthia was screaming for help, for some comfort, to make some sense out of losing her sister, her only sister, in such a brutal, tragic, and mysterious way.

Eventually, she made friends with two close pals, Katie and Angela, choosing to spend the night at their homes so that they could go out without parental oversight.

"I didn't have a lot of friends until I met Angela, after Carol died and she really went out of her way to keep me under her wing," Cynthia said.

But the parental tight control and near-paranoia continued. There was the time she was going to meet Katie in Maplecrest Park, which was on the other side of town, and Cynthia showed up late, just missing her friend.

"I called home and my mother was hysterical and then three cop cars pulled up and they surrounded me. Katie must have gone there and called my parents who called the cops," she said. "It was this big, huge thing, but it was ridiculous. My mother was crying already on the phone."

Carol's killing sent a shock through the community as well in the months that followed. It was no longer a safe town where people could come and go and leave their doors unlocked or their homes open to any visitor.

"I didn't talk about it a lot, I tried to get on with my life. It still affects me. I still will not walk anywhere by myself," said Jane Tishman, Carol's friend who lived across the street. "Once Carol passed away it was very hard for me to be in Maplewood."

For Cynthia, painting lessons in a studio above the Maplewood Theater right next to George's Luncheonette became something of a safe haven in the weeks after the killing of her sister. But that ended when her parents' overbearing interference took the fun out of it as well.

"I was always drawing and painting, but then my parents were overly interested and directing me and that was enough," she said.

Experts find the reactions of both Cynthia and her parents to be common, although damaging.

"That's normally what happened, most of the parents don't function like they did before, they barely function," said Bev Warnock, executive director of the National Organization of Parents of Murdered Children, a support group in Cincinnati. "Sometimes the siblings become the parents and have to parent them because the parents can't handle it. It is difficult to move on after the murder, especially if you don't grieve and get it out. That is what happens with a lot of men, they go to work and don't deal with it, and then the mothers have to deal with it alone and family members feel it's time to move on."

Warnock, whose group boasts thousands of parents and siblings of murdered youngsters among its members, said few will reach out for support, especially back in 1966 when the stigma was greatest.

"Back then counseling was nothing, they can't go on with their lives, they see the child's favorite food at the store or in a restaurant, they remember it was their favorite," she explained. "They did not get to see them graduate or get married. When it is a sickness, you have time to say goodbye and adjust; when it's a murder you don't know why it happened."

Connie A. Saindon, author of *The Murder Survivor's Handbook: Real-Life Stories, Tips & Resources*, agreed.

"People in those days said, 'don't keep talking about it, get over it.' The rule was you don't talk about it," she said. "It was pretty common. Nobody had information for families or victim advocates."

Saindon, who is a licensed therapist, suffered a loss similar to Cynthia Farino's, and only a few years earlier. Her younger sister, Shirley, was stabbed to death in a small town in Maine just five years before Carol was killed. The assailant was caught and tried but served just seven years in jail.

"For many years there weren't support services for co-victims because the crime victim in a homicide is deceased, so they did not see that the family were co-victims," Saindon said. "It was normal for people to withdraw because there is no support or information, the only way to cope is to emotionally close out and not talk about it.

"Emotionally, it is usually worse for the parents. Especially the mothers, they are more emotionally attached, it is not something you ever get over completely."

And the unsolved murder of a young, innocent person such as Carol deepens the hurt more because they find no justice or closure through a trial or conviction.

"If it is solved you can go to trial and get some answers. But grief is not something you learn about," Warnock said. "With a murder, they never stop grieving. They don't have any answers, they don't know what happened and they suffer more than if the person was in an accident or sick. It is the violence, it is that someone else took their lives and it is very hard to understand."

Warnock points out the guilt can be overwhelming, even if the parent did nothing wrong. In Frank Farino's case, the fact he would routinely refuse to give Carol rides and that likely caused her to walk home that night stuck with him for decades.

"They have so much guilt, asking 'Why did I let her go out? Why didn't I tell her I loved her'?" she said, mentioning another guilt-ridden mother she counseled who had forced her son to move out at 20 and was murdered in his new apartment. "The guilt is killing her because she told him to move out."

Warnock added that "the overwhelming strictness is that they don't want anything to happen to her. A lot of families don't know how to give the support, it was a whole different generation that was struggling themselves to be able to do things."

Warnock said fathers of women killed by their husbands have a similar reaction, blaming themselves for walking her down the aisle to the man who would later kill her, even if they had no reason to think he was a murderer. "I know a father of a murdered woman who will not go to weddings because it reminds him of his daughter," she said.

When tempers flared in the weeks and months after the killing, Cynthia and her parents would go at it verbally and the frustration and grief would come out in angry tirades. She said her father sometimes tried to blame her or wish she had been taken instead of the older and better-behaved Carol.

"Every time this happens in the family, they always wish the other one had died," she said. "He said that to me, he wished it was me. They idolize the one who is gone, they put them on a pedestal and the other one will never amount to that."

But Cynthia said she never blamed her sister or thought unkindly of her for leaving as some survivors often do. "No, I never felt that way, we were so close. I never felt that way, it was not her fault, my parents were nuts."

Warnock said the surviving sibling often gets the worst of it among the family members, more than the parents because she is left alone emotionally.

"We call them the forgotten survivors. When it happens the parents aren't parents anymore. It is just the natural normal thing," she said. "They don't have the feeling of family anymore. It is like losing an arm. That child can grow up very lonely not knowing what happened to her sister and she probably lost out on a good childhood or any kind of childhood with the sister."

Warnock cited a woman with two sons who lost one to murder and made a shrine on the fireplace mantel to the dead child while ignoring the one who survived.

"As he got older, he asked, 'why don't you want my picture up there?'" she said. "She wanted to memorialize him and honor him. She told us she did not realize she was doing that. When you lose something it is hard to get over that."

Warnock said many survivors like Cynthia want to find the answers and solve the mystery to help their own closure.

"We found that a lot of siblings have that goal of finding out what happened, it eats you alive. And you wonder who it was and think it could have been anybody," Warnock said.

Saindon echoed that view: "It is like a shadow of death on her, a shadow of murder. It permeates most everything."

As each day and week and month passed, Maplewood Police would continue their desperate attempts to find a lead or clues, but in many ways would try to hide the murder for the sake of the town's image, Cynthia recalls.

"They were inept at what they were doing, they had no idea what they were doing. It's like they wanted to sweep it under the rug," she said. "I think they wanted to hush it up because it was Maplewood, I am positive because the people of Maplewood back then were so snooty. They did not want it publicized because Maplewood was this place everyone wanted to move to but few could afford."

Maplewood Police Detective Christopher Dolias, who joined the department in 2014, reviewed the case at our request in 2020 and defended the police actions from 1966.

"Initially, because she didn't have any marks of struggling, that is why they thought it was someone who was known to her, so that was looked into," Dolias said. "A lot of her friends said they saw her at work because they stopped into where she was working, but nobody saw her after she went to walk home."

Dolias said there were no police cameras around town as there are now and, of course, no cell phones that might have been traced or even carry images of her attacker.

"One of the main differences is that it was normal for kids to be outside and be gone all day. Today it is more of an oddity, kids have cell phones and they are heard from and get contacted immediately," he said. "One of the problems here is that you have eyewitnesses who think they saw her in one area and have no cameras or way to be sure. So people are not sure if they saw her that day or another day."

Dolias said investigators in 1966 relied on the tight-knit community because there were more long-time residents and interpersonal communication in the small town.

"It was a completely different time. Maplewood Center was a lot different back then, right now you get a lot more people because of the train station who are not as familiar with each other," he said. "Everybody kind of knew each other, kids played together and hung out. You have a lot more residents who travel through from other communities now."

While there was no sophisticated DNA testing as there is now, police did send Carol's clothes and personal items, including the stocking that strangled her, to labs for testing to find any items or evidence left behind by the killer. Cynthia Farino recalls dog hair being found on her coat, but the family had no dog.

"They were sent out to a lab and tested for trace samples of dirt, they were looking for dog fibers and you can't really get a fingerprint from any of those objects," Dolias said. "They came back with nothing that would point to any clues toward anybody."

"One thing with this case is that Carol's father seemed strict so her not being home when she was told kind of made the parents aware that something was wrong and it just happened that the resident located her body very quickly," Dolias said. "If they did not go out to the car until the next morning, she wouldn't have been found that quickly. It could have been a different story."

He also noted that the Maplewood Police took control of such cases decades ago, unlike today when the Essex County Prosecutor's Office takes the lead.

"Back then the process was a little bit different where the agency where it occurred was primary and the prosecutor was an assisting agency. We did the primary investigation back then," the detective explained. "Now they have access to a lot more technology and a bigger budget. We don't have instances where there are murders every week, thank God, we don't need to have that technology here, it would be an economic cost."

But it also puts much of the control of the case on the prosecutor's office, which has been reluctant to provide more details on the investigation in the past 50 years and denied several requests for access to files.

Still, Dolias said police at the time believed they were able to comb as much information out of local residents and business owners as possible.

"A lot of our investigations come from relying on good relationships with business owners. They had a great relationship with the business owners, all of the officers were familiar with that area and where she worked. But that night there was a Democratic event in town. There was an influx of different people on Maplewood Avenue that day."

Dolias said the increased crowds meant that many strangers and outsiders were in Maplewood Village that night, mixing in with the residents and business owners.

"Police did tons of interviews with a lot of her friends, they went to the school and talked to lists of students," he said. "They even contacted a few of the individuals who were in the military."

But it was clear that the initial investigation did not look at the likelihood of a stranger attacking Carol, even though she worked in the restaurant at night, a place where many men frequented and anyone could have stalked her after work, as experts speculated to me.

The weekly *News-Record* also seemed to offer few updates and efforts to keep the investigation going after its initial reporting. In the six months that followed, the newspaper offered just three stories with little information and no editorials urging help with the investigation. It was as if they also wanted to keep it below the radar.

Maplewood's mayor at the time, Edmund T. Hume, appeared not to make any major effort to seek justice for the Farinos. First elected to the Township Committee in 1961, he became mayor two years later and held the top post until 1970. A World War II veteran U.S. Marine and successful executive for New Jersey Bell at the time, Hume was later appointed commissioner of the state Department of Community Affairs by former Governor William T. Cahill.

Hume also had powerful connections at the time to Congressman George M. Wallhauser, also of Maplewood, who served in Washington from 1959 to 1965, having been his campaign chairman. But it appears neither of these influential officials sought to boost the investigation.

Hume moved out of town in 1982 and spent his final years in Surf City, N.J., serving in other public positions before his death in 1996.

To add to the angst of the situation, police began to fixate on Frank Farino as a possible culprit. Despite the fact that he had been sleeping when Carol was likely killed, Cynthia recalls continued questions about his past and a clear focus on her father, to the detriment of other potential suspects or causes.

"A lot of people thought my father had done it, he was a major suspect and they wouldn't let it go, they wouldn't want to look for anyone else. He was the main focus," Cynthia remembers. "He was not a nice guy, but he didn't do it. The police were ridiculous, they would not let go of it, they thought for years that he did it. They kept trying to look for a way to pin it on him and didn't look at anyone else. I don't think he would do something like that."

It was perhaps no surprise given Frank's out-of-town past and connections to Vailsburg, with its major organized crime links. Although the Farinos were as working-class as anyone and had no mob connections as far as Cynthia knew or any records indicate, she believes there was a stigma to out-of-towners who were not White Anglo-Saxon Protestants at the time.

"My father had a very bad temper and he was abusive, but I am sure he did not do that," Cynthia said, noting police were never called to their home. "He was out looking for her at the same time they found her so they just assumed that he did it."

She said police questioned their former neighbors in Vailsburg and assumed many of them discussed his loud and violent past there as an angry father who demanded strict discipline. "One time years later he was going to hit me and I said I would tell them he killed Carol because they thought he did," Cynthia remembers.

At one point police utilized both a psychic and a hypnotist, not only for the Farinos but for some friends and associates of Carol.

A news story at the time said Police Chief Peto had turned to hypnosis "to jog the subconscious mind in the hopes the subject would recall something about an event. In the Farino case because police have not been able to find any eyewitnesses to the crime, it is hoped hypnosis would turn up forgotten associations or incidents buried in the mind of persons undergoing hypnosis."

But Cynthia saw it as more of a focus on her parents, especially her father. She said her parents were hypnotized twice, but nothing was found of substance. She claims that was more of a waste of time that could have gone toward focusing on a stranger or stalker.

"I had my doubts for a while, too," she said about her father's innocence. "But it didn't make sense to me that he would have done it or that he could have given when she died. I always wondered why they thought he did it. I knew it was because they heard of his bad temper and his abusive behavior."

Cynthia also criticized her parents for allowing the hypnotism without a lawyer present, noting the police took advantage of their naivete about such practices.

"They should have had an attorney, they were very trusting," Cynthia said. "The police kept thinking that my father had done it. They even threatened to dig up my backyard because they never found her purse or her shoes. My parents were pushed around all over the place."

Det. Dolias confirmed the psychic and hypnotism, describing one of them as a "transvoyant."

"That was a different style of police work at the time. They would question him and she would tell them and say when she thought he was lying, kind of like a human lie detector," Dolias said. "She would talk about where her missing shoes or purse might be and they were cooperative."

He also defended the focus on the family and friends, contending they did not take away from other investigative avenues: "I don't know if that was a detriment to anything else."

Cynthia remembers the police calling her parents in multiple times for questioning in a way that seemed unusual and without any specific purpose other than to grill them further and possibly get one of them to slip up and admit something incriminating.

"They would just call them up and have them come down and after a while, I thought 'This is not right.' It finally dawned on them that he was a suspect," Cynthia said. "It was then they stopped cooperating."

The Farinos became so frustrated with the police efforts that they soon found a private investigator.

Phil Burberick was a private detective who offered his services to the Farinos at no cost. Cynthia later understood why as his tactics were sometimes impacted by a drinking problem.

But she still gave him more credit than the police because he seemed to believe her father had not done the killing and other areas needed to be explored.

"I think he gained more of an understanding of what [Carol] was like. He said my parents didn't know their daughter the way they thought they did," Cynthia said. "He didn't think it was my father at all. He approached my parents because, I think, he realized [the police] were focusing on my dad and not anything else."

Cynthia remembers Burberick bringing groups of Carol's friends to the house for questioning and asking them what they knew about Carol and her social life.

"One night he came over and had all her friends show up and had them all talk for hours," she said. "He tried to see if someone saw something and get at what she was like, the cops never did any of that."

But Cynthia, who knew much more about her sister than a lot of the friends, was kept out of the discussions. She said one time she was sent to a friend's house when the interviews occurred.

"I would sit on a window seat at the top of the stairs and listen, that was how I would hear things and learn things," she said. "That's how I gained information."

The family found Burberick to be a good person, who tried and put his total effort into the case. He came over regularly to update them and grew close to the family.

But as the weeks passed, the Farinos and police were no closer to finding Carol's killer than they were on day one. And the pressure was mounting. Pressure on the police to solve the crime, on the family to come to grips with their loss, and on Cynthia Farino to "get over it."

But she only felt more anger, distrust, and resentment for her parents for failing to support her, for her school for treating her as some kind of freak, and for the police for not bringing her sister justice.

"I became a very angry adolescent," she said. "I didn't trust anybody."

Chapter Seven

It was less than a year after Carol Ann Farino's murder that Richard Cottingham committed his first brutal slaying. That close time proximity and similarities between the crimes were enough to make him among the first potential suspects years later.

Cottingham, who was only two years older than Carol, was born in The Bronx, but grew up in River Vale, N.J., just 30 miles up the Garden State Parkway from Maplewood. He graduated from Pascack Valley High School in 1964, three years before Carol would have received her Columbia High School diploma.

Outwardly, Cottingham—the oldest of three children—was a friendly, popular, good-looking young man who earned a reputation for attracting pretty young women. That asset would prove deadly for many of his targets who fell victim to his charms and, later, to his murderous ways.

He would eventually be convicted of killing nine young women, but claims to have murdered nearly 100. In many cases, the victims were not only brutally slaughtered but many were sexually assaulted and even dismembered, earning Cottingham the nickname, "The Torso Killer."

Several were also strangled to death in a style eerily similar to Carol's killer.

Although he was shy and awkward as a student at St. Andrews School in Westwood, N.J., Cottingham gained more friends and confidence in high school where he excelled on the athletic field and later became a leader of a small circle of athletic acquaintances.

"That would be normal for a psychopath with grandiose ideas about themselves," true crime author Jack Rosewood wrote in his book, *The Torso Killer*, about Cottingham. "That usually leans toward narcissism. It's just that others never really saw him in the same light."

High school friends tell Rosewood that Cottingham didn't really stand out in any notable way, other than being somewhat reserved and "removed from the mainstream," as one friend told *The Record* of Bergen County.

But several classmates said he would speak disparagingly of women and boasted a breast fetish, Rosewood writes: "In Cottingham's case, those large breasts he coveted would eventually become fetishized, a paraphilia necessary for arousal."

After high school, Cottingham went to work with his father for Met Life Insurance as a computer operator and had taken a similar job with Blue Cross and Blue Shield in New York City just months before Carol was killed.

But police never suspected or arrested Cottingham for any of his crimes until 1980, when he was charged with attempted murder and sexual assault of a woman in a motel in Hasbrouck Heights, N.J., not far from his hometown.

That later connected him to several earlier slayings dating back to 1977 of women in the same motel, including at least one who was strangled, news reports indicate. Eventually, he would be convicted of several prostitute murders in New York City in the 1970s and '80s, along with a handful of other young women in New Jersey.

He is serving more than 200 years in New Jersey State Prison in Trenton.

"A man who was also gifted with the tendencies of a narcissist who felt that he was above the world, Cottingham believed that his needs trumped those of others," Rosewood wrote. "So he had no trouble seeing his victims as little more than toys put on earth solely to fulfill his own sadistic desires."

After being convicted of five murders by 1984 and sentenced to more than 20 years behind bars, Cottingham then began confessing to other killings that police had not even sought to link to him.

Most recently, in January 2020, he claimed to have been responsible for three older murders with some similarities to Carol Ann Farino, most notably that the victims were teen girls, with dark hair, and all murdered by strangulation in the late 1960s.

The Daily Voice of Hackensack reported on Jan. 3, 2020, that those Cottingham claimed to have killed included:

• Jacalyn (Jackie) Harp, 13, of Midland Park, who was walking home from school band practice on July 17, 1968, when she was strangled with the leather strap of her flag sling;

• Irene Blase, 18, of Bogota, who went missing from Hackensack on April 7, 1969 "and was found face-down in four feet of water in Saddle River, strangled with a wire, cord, or perhaps the chain of a crucifix she was wearing."

• Denise Falasca, 15, of Closter, who went missing from Westwood on July 14, 1969 "and was found the next morning in Saddle Brook by the side of a road next to a cemetery, strangled with a cord or the chain of her crucifix."

But the closest Cottingham link to Carol Ann Farino is the murder of Nancy Schiava Vogel, 29, whose strangled body was found in her car on Oct. 30, 1967, in Little Ferry, N.J. Like his other victims, she was young and dark-haired, but someone he had known as a neighbor in the same apartment complex.

She was also killed less than a year after Carol.

Police were led to Vogel's murder by Cottingham when he confessed in September 2010, more than 40 years after her death. *The Record* reported the confession on Sept. 19, 2010, more than a month after it happened, noting he "quietly pleaded guilty" to the killing in August of that year.

Bergen County Prosecutor John Molinelli told the newspaper the confession and subsequent closure of the case followed many conversations and visits with Cottingham, who remains incarcerated at New Jersey State Prison. He said it was "the culmination of years of traveling to the prison" to speak with Cottingham until he confessed and it could be verified through other evidence and detective work.

Vogel, a married mother of two, was last seen alive on the night of Friday, Oct. 27, 1967, when she told her husband of nine years, Henry, that she was going to play bingo at St. Margaret Roman Catholic Church in Little Ferry.

"Henry wasn't worried because bingo was a regular tradition in the predominantly Italian Catholic neighborhood," Rosewood wrote. "But when the late-night news was over and Nancy still wasn't home, he started to worry."

Her husband reported her missing the next day after she failed to appear at the family's front door in the morning. Two days later, on Monday, her body was found beaten and strangled in her 1960 Rambler on Homestead Avenue in neighboring Ridgefield Park.

The location is about a mile and a half from the church, the same distance that Carol Ann Farino's body was taken from her last known location to where her dead body was found.

News reports at the time indicated the car and body were spotted by two 12-year-old girls who had just gotten home from St. Francis Parochial School and were looking out the window. They approached the car to investigate after thinking it was a mannequin but informed neighbors when they saw it was a dead body.

Vogel was found naked with her hands tied in front of her by a thin nylon cord and her clothes folded and placed under her body. Police later determined she had never gotten to the bingo game and had ended up shopping at Valley Fair Mall in Little Ferry after packages from the mall purchased on Oct. 27 were found in the trunk—two pairs of shoes and a blouse.

As in Carol's case, police focused on people who knew Vogel and sought witnesses around her neighborhood and at the mall, including one man who told them he saw her talking to two men. But none of the leads ever resulted in a suspect or an arrest.

Rosewood contends that Vogel might have been lured by Cottingham's charm and young good looks either at the mall or outside as she returned to her car.

"The two both lived in Little Ferry and Nancy likely thought little of it when Cottingham approached her car after running into her at the mall," he wrote in his book. "It might have been easy to talk her into driving somewhere other than bingo, given his silver-tongued approach to attracting his victims."

Prosecutor Molinelli confirmed that Vogel and Cottingham likely knew each other and it would not have been a surprise if he asked for a ride and she agreed. "He did murder her in the vehicle and then park the vehicle," the prosecutor said about the killer of Vogel.

Cottingham would turn 21 a month later and go on to commit several similar killings before his 25th birthday, all young, brunette women strangled to death and left for dead. But none of those initial murders would ever be discovered until he confessed to them more than 50 years after.

Instead, he led a life like any other young man in the late 1960s, working his way up as a computer operator and marrying his wife, Janet, in 1970. By 1976, they had three children and lived moderately in Little Ferry and then in Lodi, N.J., just four miles west.

But the entire time Cottingham's mind went to a dark place, according to co-workers. One fellow computer staffer, Dominick Volpe, told Rosewood he would talk about "crazy things" like his obsession with gambling, prostitutes, and sadomasochistic activities. "He was very upfront about it, he liked the slave thing, handcuffs. He was a gambler and he was not afraid to take chances on anything."

He also got into some smaller scrapes with the law, including a 1972 shoplifting charge that led to a $50 fine and an assault and robbery charge in 1973 that was later dropped.

Then the affairs started. Multiple accounts in books and news reports alleged Cottingham had several girlfriends between 1973 and 1980 when he was first arrested in Hasbrouck Heights for the attempted murder of an 18-year-old prostitute at a motel.

Janet Cottingham filed for divorce in 1979, according to *The Record*, claiming in her complaint that Cottingham would leave the family without money and return early in the morning on many days. It also said he visited Plato's Retreat, a Manhattan swingers' club.

By the end of May 1980, police had linked Cottingham to several other New Jersey murders of young women, as well as a handful of prostitute killings in New York City. In all, he was later convicted of killing five women in both places between 1977 and 1980, one more brutal than the next.

After his initial four killings in the 1960s involved mostly beatings and strangulation of young New Jersey women, he later graduated to sadistic mutilation and dismemberment, according to news reports.

In 1977, he lured Maryann Carr, 26, into his car in Little Ferry and took her to a Quality Inn in Hasbrouck Heights where he tortured and strangled her before dumping her body in the parking lot. Like Carol Ann Farino, her purse and shoes were missing.

The first of the prostitute killings occurred on Dec. 2, 1979, when two bodies were recovered from a Times Square hotel that had been set on fire. Firefighters later found two beheaded bodies that had also had their hands removed.

It was eventually determined that Cottingham fled with the hands and heads and had doused the torsos with lighter fluid before setting them ablaze. Those victims included Deedeh Goodarzi, 22, and another woman who was never identified.

One of the responding firefighters was so distraught by the images that he considered trauma counseling, according to Rod Leith, a former Record reporter who covered Cottingham's murders and compiled the New York killings in a book titled *The Prostitute Murders.*

"On the street that cold winter day word of the bloody torso slayings sent an extra chill down the spines of a certain group of working women," Leith wrote in his book. "It didn't take long for these streetwise ladies to figure out who those two women were and what they were doing in that hotel at 515 West 42nd Street."

Times Square was a different place in the 1970s and early 1980s, as was most of Manhattan. Crime rates were skyrocketing and the city's drug, murder, and violence rates were at record levels. The area of low-rent hotels was a den of prostitution, pickpockets, and seedy dives where hookers could make a living more openly than today.

"The person responsible for the torso murders became the number one target of a massive dragnet conducted by the New York Police Department," Leith wrote. "No stone would be left unturned. A task force of detectives was put on the city's biggest manhunt. So determined were the police in their search for the murderer that the task force included deep-sea divers, assigned to plunge into the chilly waters of the Hudson River and other waterways around Manhattan and the Metropolitan Area in the seemingly fruitless hunt for the heads and hands of the victims."

As Cottingham's interest in sex, abuse, and torture of women grew, the streetwalking trade in Manhattan served his needs well. He could venture into New York City, lure a young hooker out with money and charm, and finish her off with his sick abusive fantasies, then travel back home to New Jersey.

"I always had the ability to attract women," Cottingham confessed to Nadia Fezzani, a Canadian journalist who is one of the few reporters to interview him at any length. "You know, it's one of those things you can't explain. If I went to a bar, very rarely would I walk out without a woman. Because I would understand the psychiatry, the psychological effect of how to pick up women, what they were looking for. I would always go to the prettiest ones because most men were afraid and they'd go to the average-looking girl or the average one."

He later told Fezzani that he took pleasure in torturing his victims: "I enjoyed it, it was a game. It's scary to a girl to have something done like that, to be so close to a knife pressed against you." He called it "a power trip, the power of holding someone's fate in your hand is an aphrodisiac. It is God-like."

"I had nerves of steel," Cottingham added when asked about getting away with the killings for so long. He cited one instance when he was carrying the heads of two victims out of a motel and police stopped him and never asked to inspect the bag he was carrying or ask for I.D.: "People believe what they want to believe."

Cottingham returned to killing on May 4, 1980, when he picked up prostitute Valorie Ann Street, 19, in New York and took her to the same New Jersey Quality Inn where he had dumped Carr's body. There he tortured and murdered her, later stuffing her body under the bed where a maid found her.

Just 11 days later he struck again, on May 15, 1980, when Mary Ann Renyer, 25, was found stabbed, mutilated, and strangled in the Hotel Seville on East 29th Street, near Fifth Avenue, in Manhattan.

During that three-year span, Cottingham also attacked several other women who got away, some with mutilations that included having their nipples bitten off. Several would go on to testify against him in his 1981 trial for one of the murders and four other related killings.

One of those survivors was Leslie Ann O'Dell, 18, who was attacked and tortured for hours by Cottingham on May 22, 1980, according to Leith. He writes that the prostitute, who came to New York from Washington State via bus just a few days earlier, had no money and was looking for a new life after a fight with her boyfriend.

Like many young women arriving desperate and poor at New York's Port Authority Bus Terminal at the time, O'Dell was approached by an opportunistic pimp who quickly bought her breakfast and offered to help.

Soon she was walking the streets where Cottingham approached her in his blue and silver Chevrolet Caprice at the corner of Lexington Avenue and 25th Street. After some friendly chatter, they went to a bar and shared drinks. Cottingham, using the name Tommy, then suggested they go to New Jersey, where he lived.

During the night they drove, ate at a roadside diner, and finally arrived at the same Quality Inn in Hasbrouck Heights where two of Cottingham's previous victims had met their deaths.

After paying the $27 hotel fee, Cottingham and O'Dell went to Room 117 where they climbed into bed and began what she thought would be a typical paid sex encounter. But when he told her to roll onto her stomach and began handcuffing her from behind, she realized it was a mistake.

"He told me to shut up, that I was a whore and I had to be punished," O'Dell later testified, according to *The New York Times*. "He said the other girls took it and I had to take it, too. He said that uncountable times."

Leith writes that Cottingham pulled out a knife and held it to O'Dell's throat, ordering her not to scream: "She fought back the desperate need to scream as he told her he was going to beat her very badly, cut her, and leave scars on her face, her breasts, her vagina, and her anus. He was going to cut her uncountable times. Just too many times, he threatened."

Cottingham then went on to sodomize her twice and pulled out a belt to beat her, telling her again and again she had to be punished for being a prostitute. He stopped briefly, even wiping her face in a gentle, caressing way, before pulling out a pistol and another set of handcuffs to place on her ankles, Leith revealed. He said if she did not do what he said he would shoot her.

"She pleaded again, but he just got more and more enraged, telling her to shut up," Leith recounted. "He was going to torture her some more. She had to let him do whatever he wanted to her. If she let one more word out, he would put a bullet in her head."

He then laid down on the bed next to her and took the cuffs off her ankles, forcing her to perform oral sex on him and other acts with her tongue. At one point, Cottingham turned over on his stomach and pushed O'Dell on the floor to do more acts on his toes. While down there, she later revealed she felt around and got his gun out of the leather case he had brought.

When he turned over again, she pointed the gun at Cottingham and pulled the trigger, twice, but nothing happened. That's when he pulled out his knife again and went after her with it. "Oh God, no, Oh God!" she screamed.

A maid in the hallway heard the screams and approached Room 117, but did not knock or try to get in, recalling that a murder had occurred there just months earlier. Instead, the housekeeper informed the front desk.

Back in the room, Cottingham was angrier than ever at O'Dell's attention-getting screams. Just as he threatened to kill her again, the phone rang. It was the motel's assistant manager and the head housekeeper asking about the screams. O'Dell tried to appear calm to placate Cottingham, but the hotel staffers knew something was up and sent security to the room.

When they arrived, O'Dell went to the door but kept the chain on as Cottingham directed while holding a knife to her back. When she answered, the assistant manager and head housekeeper could see she was puffy-eyed and bruised, but she would not let them in.

They left for the office and called the room again, prompting O'Dell to answer and lie that she was fine and had only had a fight with her boyfriend. She then hung up and fell onto the bed as Cottingham grew angrier.

The assistant manager waited no longer and called the police, who pulled up as Cottingham sought to pack up his items and leave. He forgot about his victim, running out the door and down the hall as O'Dell screamed for people to stop him: "He tried to kill me."

Cottingham eventually reached the first floor and was running toward the rear motel entrance when Hasbrouck Heights Police Officer Stanley Melowic entered the building with a loaded 12-gauge shotgun.

He ordered Cottingham to stop and raised the weapon just as the suspect halted inches from the deadly firearm. He didn't even wait to be ordered and put his hands up against the wall to await his arrest and handcuffing.

Finally, 13 years after killing his first known victim, Richard Cottingham was caught and would never be freed again.

During his interrogation, Cottingham stuck to his story that the incident was just a consensual prostitution act and used the skills he had perfected over the years of staying calm and acting as if nothing was wrong.

Eventually, however, he opened up about his motives and obsession, police said later.

"I was holding his hand and trying to get him to confess," said former Detective Ed Denning, who along with his partner, Detective Alan Greico, pursued the case. "And his eyes welled up and he became red and said, 'I have a problem with women'. But then that was the end of the interview, he refused to talk after that."

But when police searched his home they found much of the evidence they would need to convict him of the O'Dell attack and many of the previous murders. Key among the evidence was a so-called "Trophy Room" where Cottingham kept souvenirs of his abuse and murder.

Rod Leith wrote that it was a "collection of mysterious items in the basement of the Cottingham home." Among them were women's clothing, jewelry, perfume, motel keys, and purses.

Cottingham's wife, Janet, was in the house when they executed the search warrant and she showed surprise at the items. She would later reveal that she had suspected Cottingham was doing something nefarious, since he often stayed out into the early morning hours, although her mind never wandered to a potential murder spree.

As Carol Ann Farino's murder remained unsolved, Cottingham was a potential suspect in her case given the similarities and location of her death, his first known victim, and the close timeline.

Hearing of his arrest soon after, Cynthia Farino could not help but wonder if he had been the culprit that took her sister's life.

"I was watching a show about him and I realized that it was strangulation and that he was a possibility," Cynthia said. "He was very charming, it said, and he could make women feel comfortable. Maybe he came into the luncheonette and [Carol] talked to him, that sparked my interest because he was North Jersey and he strangled them. It was another avenue that hadn't been looked into, it was another person that could be a suspect and was not considered."

She even admitted that the belief Carol would not get into a car with a stranger might have been premature given Cottingham's ability to lure and seduce young women. "Maybe he talked to her at the luncheonette and he made her feel comfortable with him."

Other experts of local serial murders and the Cottingham case found Carol's killing similar enough to Cottingham's earlier murders—involving strangulation of young, dark-haired women—that one had to consider a connection.

Among them is Rod Leith, who speculated in a 2020 interview that Carol's murder had enough Cottingham-like elements to make him suspect. He said Cottingham worked in insurance at the time and may have been in nearby Newark on business, stopping at the Maplewood eatery where Carol worked for a late supper.

"He tended to take shifts that were late, insurance-related," Leith told me. "He preferred to work the off hours and he would work late night and early morning and peruse the areas that he worked in for women. He would have been single and it depends on what his routine was."

Leith said Cottingham may have been dating someone near Newark and the couple could have been in Maplewood for a movie or other event and stopped in at Milt's Cup and Saucer while waiting for the nearby train or as a quick dinner spot.

Given Cottingham's past practice of luring young women, seeing the young and attractive Carol could have drawn Cottingham to return later or on another night.

"What might take him down to that area is if he was dating somebody and they may have stopped into that diner for that reason, maybe they stopped off there," Leith speculated. "He may have been working in Newark and coming back he could have stopped off after work."

Vernon Geberth, the former New York City detective turned author who worked on several of Cottingham's prostitute killings, also said his initial New Jersey murders mirrored Carol's death enough to consider him.

"You can't assume anything," Geberth declared. "He recently confessed to three murders that nobody knew about. There are some similarities, he did strangle all of his victims. He was a predator and a half. We did not become aware of him until 1979."

That delay in tying him to the three New Jersey killings in the late 1960s and the first one in 1967 would hamper connecting Cottingham to other murders, such as Carol's, that occurred so long ago.

But the similarities in actions, location, and timeframe make Cottingham hard to ignore as a suspect.

Although he has confessed to killings never before linked to him, including dozens that have yet to be proven, investigators say it is still unclear what to believe or not when he decides to come clean. "I talked to him once myself, it was like head games," Geberth said.

The most knowledgeable person about Richard Cottingham may be Peter Vronsky, a New Jersey-based author and investigator who has penned several books on serial killers. He maintains an elaborate database of area killings and victims.

Vronsky also has a long-running relationship with Cottingham and is credited with helping to unlock some of his recent confessions.

He also believes Cottingham killed Carol Ann Farino.

"It is 90% likely that it is him," Vronsky told me in a 2020 phone interview. "He clearly has a fetish for nurses. The one thing that might have drawn him to her was the white waitress uniform."

Carol was found with her uniform on and her shoes were missing, another Cottingham trait in his early killings. She was also strangled, as were Cottingham's first four known victims.

"He looks very good for this one. Partly it meets his profile, the kind of victim he likes. These meet his victim preferences in that period, in the 1960s, the kind of randomness of it," Vronsky said. "There was a vehicle used, the quick way she was killed was very similar to the Jacqueline

Harp murder. She was killed within 10 or 15 minutes of her encounter with Cottingham."

I came across Vronsky after writing to Cottingham seeking an interview. He passed on my request to Vronsky, who said the convicted killer did not want to speak but allowed him to do so on his behalf.

Vronsky already knew about Farino's murder and believed it could fit Cottingham's profile for some of the same reasons Leith and Geberth pointed to him. Vronsky said he has asked Cottingham about Farino, but he would not confirm or deny.

"He is 73 years old so his memory is problematic," Vronsky said. "When I brought up a diner waitress dressed in white, there was kind of reaction from him that he remembered something like that. He often drove around at random. But he probably would not remember if he was in Maplewood."

Vronsky also speculated that the killing was quick and did not involve rape penetration because Cottingham may have been unable to maintain an erection, choosing to kill her out of frustration and anger: "It is not atypical, a lot of serial killers cannot complete the act."

Maplewood Police Detective Dolias said Cottingham's name did come up in the ongoing investigation of Carol's murder, but police could not make anything stick: "He was mentioned and talked about as a potential suspect, but they didn't have anything to tie him down."

Chapter Eight

Thanksgiving 1966 took place exactly three weeks after Carol Ann Farino's murder. Her family had very little for which to be thankful. Stress, depression, and frustration over a lack of closure, slow police work, and growing guilt by Frank and Ann Farino permeated the household.

And Cynthia Farino was often the center of the focus.

"I always felt like I had to be good so my parents wouldn't get upset and I had to walk on eggshells all the time around them," Cynthia said. "My dad had his temper so I didn't know when he was going to go off."

They did manage to have a semblance of Thanksgiving due to the generosity of next-door neighbor Janet Smith, a kindly older woman who had no immediate family, but what seemed like a dozen cats.

"Otherwise we would not have had Thanksgiving, she had us over," Cynthia recalls. "Her cats would always wander over to our yard and I adopted one of them and he sort of became our cat."

"It was something that made me happy because I got to play with the cats and later I would sit up in my bedroom and I used to look out the window and watch them."

Janet Smith offered a friendly image for Cynthia as she peered out her bedroom window and often played with a few of the cats when they would venture into the Farinos' yard. The 12-year-old's life was a whirlwind of loss, shock, anger, and distrust.

Sometimes Cynthia would go into Carol's second-floor bedroom, which her parents kept just as it was on the night she died, and watch Janet feeding her cats through her kitchen window.

"I used to go in her room and sit on the bed, I could see down into her kitchen and she would feed them the plates on the floor," Cynthia recalls. "I liked to look out at them, it was something I could do to feel better."

Janet offered as much comfort as she could on that holiday, setting up a typical Thanksgiving spread with turkey and the trimmings. She tried to keep the chat upbeat and friendly, but Ann and Frank could only manage pleasantries.

The friendly neighbor found herself in the same uncertain place as most of those who knew the Farinos. People don't know how to act and the relatives of those lost feel unsure as well.

And when it's a holiday, there is a reminder that someone is missing. That loss of place, especially at a holiday dinner table, drives home the sadness even more. Celebrating Thanksgiving at someone else's house might have taken some of the sting out, experts say.

"One thing you can do is start some new tradition that is so different from old celebrations that it has no painful memories for you," author and grief counselor Helen Fitzgerald wrote in *The Mourning Handbook*.

The Thanksgiving dinner offered a generous respite for the Farinos, but the grief and negative feelings returned soon after and continued through Christmas of that year.

"We were big on Christmas, but after that, it was not good," Cynthia said. "That year we didn't have a tree, we didn't do anything."

She asked her parents why they had no tree, decorations, or other Christmas traditions.

"My father was screaming at me, 'how can you want that?'" she recalled. "He would yell and scream because I would even ask. He would yell at me, 'What's wrong with you? Don't you miss your sister?' I would want to yell at him. I didn't have Christmas. My mother put a little Christmas tree in my room, but that was it."

It was a far cry from most years when the family did the holiday season in a big way: "We'd have a big Christmas tree and we'd decorate it on Christmas Eve. That was a tradition, everything else was ready to go. My father was so perfectionist, you had to put the tinsel on one strand at a time, not in clumps."

As 1966 turned into 1967, the family dysfunction continued, with police offering few leads and Ann and Frank mixing guilt with efforts to express their anger, but no ability to seek help or admit they needed it.

Carol Ann Farino

"He felt so guilty about it he blamed himself and my mother did, too," Cynthia recalls about her father. "When he would pick her up from work, she would tell him, 'Oh, you learned your lesson, you're on time for a change.'"

As for Cynthia, seventh grade continued with a mix of unknowns about her parents, her future, and what happened to her sister. She trudged through that first year of junior high school, but with some unusual reactions from others.

"Junior high was a blur to me. I don't remember a lot about that year. I remember my mother was taking sedatives and she passed out at dinner once, her head hit the table," she said. "I never went out with a lot of people because my father wouldn't let me and he would never take me anywhere. Sometimes if I went with a friend their parents would take us. But that was it."

In school, Cynthia became the invisible girl to classmates and those in charge.

"Everybody runs for the hills, they stay away from you. People would avoid me rather than sit and talk to me after it all happened. My teachers were very bizarre to me," Cynthia said. "They were not demanding if I didn't do my homework. No one would say anything, I felt very isolated and teachers wanted to avoid me at all costs."

Most days were spent walking the half-mile to school through Memorial Park, then back home, with no afterschool activities.

"I didn't do anything socially, nothing. I had to go home right after school," Cynthia said. "I would do my homework and go up in my room and listen to music and watched TV."

While Carol had been a doo-wop and teen idol fan, Cynthia's musical taste turned toward the more outspoken and experimental music that was unfolding in the late 1960s and early 1970s. The Beatles' "White Album" was a favorite, along with The Rolling Stones, The Doors, Jimi Hendrix, and Janis Joplin.

She recalls going to see James Brown live in concert and fearing her parents would find out and come down hard with a punishment. "I never told my parents where I went because my father would have had a stroke. I remember I wasn't supposed to be there. The show was amazing."

As the months went on, Cynthia stayed home more and formed a unique relationship with Ann watching television. The duo would relax after school or at night in front of the TV once housework and homework were done.

"I had to watch what she wanted, but my mother and I liked the same things," Cynthia recalls. "We would watch a lot of old movies together, that's why I got hooked on them." Natalie Wood was a favorite in the 1960s dramas *Love With a Proper Stranger* and *This Property is Condemned*.

"Whatever was on the Million Dollar Movie," she noted about the local New York area classic film series on local station WOR-TV. "But no soap operas. My mother hated all of that crap. My mother didn't drive so she was home all the time."

All through that first year after Carol's death, the family felt under watch as police seemed to focus on Frank Farino and avoid other potential suspects.

"I only heard what my parents discovered and that's how I got all of the information," she said, noting that the private investigator they hired would check in with cops, but got few details. "As far as I knew through junior high school they were after my dad. He would go around Maplewood asking stupid questions, talking to [Carol's] friends and I think made himself look suspect. They wouldn't tell us anything after a while because they thought it was him."

She recalls her father being stopped for a routine traffic incident on Boyden Avenue near Irvington and the situation escalating to a point where four police cars arrived and gave him a major grilling.

"It was harassment, they just made him look ridiculous," Cynthia said. "It was such a stupid thing."

And her extended family was no help. Cynthia said neither her mother nor father's siblings or relatives offered much support, likely because they did not know what to do.

"My mother's family was never around after that year," she remembered. "I don't think we ever did anything that year with anybody. I'm not a cold person, sometimes I lack empathy for other people and I think it's because of what I went through."

A mix of Ann and Frank's over-protective approach and lack of sympathy for what Cynthia was going through following Carol's death made her situation increasingly stressful and upsetting.

"I was angry, I got very angry and I became a very good liar because I had to lie to them about what I was doing," she said. "It was such a constant frustration that they were on top of everything, they wanted to ask all the time what I did."

She recalls her parents forbidding her to go see *Carnal Knowledge*, the controversial 1971 R-rated movie about free sexual activity among four college friends. "I couldn't do a lot of things and be out. I couldn't even go to the movies sometimes. They wouldn't let me go to that movie."

Such mixed emotions for a surviving family are not unusual, says Sherry Horacek, a licensed professional therapist and grief counselor. And in the late 1960s, the lack of options and the continued stigma for outside help only made it worse.

"In the 60s, there were psychiatrists and therapists, but in-grief counseling was probably rare if it existed," Horacek said, adding that Ann and Frank were dealing with a mix of guilt and grief that they would take out on Cynthia. "There is the thing that your job is to keep your child safe and I didn't so there is guilt, so I have to keep this one safe. So I keep them safe by not letting them do anything."

"The anger at everything comes up when you are grieving, especially when it is a child. There is anger at God, at police, at anything, and that can spill over into everything around you. You take it out on the people you care about. A lot of anger spilling over all over the place here. You can find myriad reasons to feel guilty when your child dies, and it can eat you alive."

And when her parents did not provide the proper support for Cynthia after Carol's death, it affected her in a wide variety of ways—from loneliness to anger to stress.

"There has got to be trauma around that," Horacek explained. "If you are a 12-year-old and your sister is murdered and there is no solace to be found from your parents, that is difficult. There probably was no solace to be had and it doesn't sound like things improved with time."

But Cynthia soldiered on, continuing with seventh and eighth grade and allowing herself to survive and seek some positive outlets and hope for the future.

Two of her closest friends during that time were Angela Caruso and Gabriela "Gabe" Bogden. Gabe had met Cynthia in fifth grade at Fielding School, which is now the school district office. Angela recalls their first meeting in seventh grade.

"We went all through middle school and high school," Gabe said in 2020. "I am sure it was tough. It was definitely weird even when I went over because of all the talk about the father. I would go to her house. She was not close to her father. I am sure when she was home around her family, it was a lot harder."

She said the friends would still get out and about and have fun socializing, often just to get away from Cynthia's family.

"We used to hang out in Maplewood Village," Gabe said. "We used to hang out there because they had the booths and the jukebox, but not much more. That is why I think she got married at a young age, her parents being so strict on her."

Angela remembers the girls coming together in seventh grade and staying friends through the end of high school. She recalls Cynthia being positive and upbeat—more than one might expect given her situation—and never bringing up the dark subject that was probably on a lot of minds.

"We met that year when Carol died, being 12 years old we never spoke about it, it never got talked about," Angela said. "I remember that it had happened. But we never really hung out in her home, it was not that kind of home, not a lot of happiness. We kind of hung out at our house, but we never brought it up or spoke about it. I don't recall having a conversation about it."

She said Carol's friends also knew that police remained focused on

Frank Farino, even with no real evidence, creating even more uncertainties in their minds.

"I knew her father was a suspect, but we did not know what it was like at home. I think it had to be rough for her," Angela said. "We were just kids and did the minimal things. I knew she wasn't comfortable in her own home and wasn't happy there."

Cynthia recalls the two friends, and a third girl, Katie Jantzen, who befriended her as well. She said the four of them became a tight group that helped her get through her upper-class years.

"I didn't have any real good friends until I met Angela and Katie and Gabe," she said. "Then we were all inseparable. They were my best friends, I started hanging out with them in eighth or ninth grade. I didn't hang out with a lot of people in seventh grade, I think people didn't know what to do, they treated me strangely."

Gabe admits she and others did not know how to treat Cynthia initially, given the brutal killing and the cloud of suspicion hanging over her father. But after a while, they ended up doing the same things most teens did.

"We went to some church dances, but neither of us was into more than that, we wanted to hang around," Gabe said. "In the early part, yeah, everybody knew that it happened. It was a devastating thing through the whole time. We were still kind of young, we didn't know what death was, really. I remember in high school we later found out the story, where they found her body and the other stuff. She was maybe a little more reserved than the rest of us, but I think the whole situation had a lot of impact on her."

Cynthia also found her first boyfriend sometime in junior high school, perhaps late seventh or eighth grade. She's not sure exactly when but Fred was a nice guy, which she needed at the time.

In a junior high school of the late 1960s, of course, having a boyfriend meant maybe walking to and from school and talking on the phone, not much more.

"We were in the same class and I really liked going out with him," she said. "My parents made me break up with him, I was embarrassed to tell him. He was so nice. We used to talk on the phone and we would go to some places, but not very often."

By early 1968, Frank and Ann Farino had had enough of 5 Jefferson Avenue—too many bad memories, especially when the suspicion over Frank's involvement in Carol's killing remained. Cynthia does not recall her father ever officially being dropped as a suspect.

"I thought police had information that I didn't know about my father, I thought for a long time he had done it, or might have done it. I was never really sure until later," she said. "I didn't know exactly what happened because I couldn't get any information. I thought they just knew something I didn't know about him. But I now know he didn't do it."

So about 18 months after Carol's murder the family moved across town to 28 Orchard Road, closer to Irvington and farther from both Maplewood Junior High School and Columbia High School.

"My father hated it [on Jefferson Avenue] because he had to share a driveway and the person next door rented out the second floor and the tenants had to use it and I think he was miserable there," Cynthia said. "It was a real reminder for the both of them."

But she liked her old house, especially the neighbor's cats. "The other house was pretty tight, but it had a lot of charm."

The Farinos had found another house on Parker Avenue, close to both schools and the Jefferson Avenue home, but lost it in what they assumed was an anti-Italian discrimination move—not uncommon at the time in such a WASPy community.

"I don't think they wanted to sell it to us, there was still a lot of anti-Italian feeling," Cynthia recalled.

Cynthia entered Columbia High School in the fall of 1969, almost four years after Carol's death. Walking the same halls her sister did at the time of her death, and with an entirely new group of classmates from South Orange Middle School blending in, she once again had to deal with the same stares and weird questions as the sister of the murder victim whose killing was still unsolved.

Even though years had passed, the cops were no closer to any answers than they were when it occurred.

Columbia High School was changing, however. Even in the time between Carol's first day and Cynthia's entrance, the large red brick building had seen the influx of long hair, civil rights, as well as anti-war and pro-drug views among its more than 2,000 students.

The school experienced both vandalism and the opening of smoking sections for students—including some in student rest rooms. The teens also launched the school's first underground magazine.

For Cynthia, it was a new world of options and more friends, but with lingering anger and sadness.

"It was different and I had no problem picking up on school things, but I was just depressed, I had underlying depression," she admits. "My grades were good, and I knew I was smart, but I didn't excel the way I should have because I was miserable all the time. I think it was everything that clouded over us. I was able to get out a bit more at least."

She also spent more time out of the house when possible and with Angela, Gabe, and Katie Jantzen. Many weekend nights were spent with the foursome camped out in Angela's bedroom.

"It was all about boys," Angela recalls about their sleepover bull sessions. "We would go to the beach and lay in the sun and fry up. We never really went to the city until after high school. We would drink in the park and go to dances and hang out at each other's houses, play spin the bottle."

Angela said of Cynthia at the time: "I think she looked at things more negatively back then.

"We didn't date back then, everybody hung out," Cynthia recalls, although she had a boyfriend of sorts her first years in high school, "Keith someone or other. He was more of a friend," she said. "I went out with him for quite a while, then he became a Jesus freak, but he was Jewish. He was a nice guy."

But Cynthia still wrestled with depression and anger demons as her sister's death remained unsolved and her parents grew more distant and strict. At one point, in the summer of 1971, she closed off completely and never went out for months—no dates, no parties, and very little outside contact.

"I was tired of arguing with my parents and feeling like I couldn't do anything, didn't talk to anyone," she remembers. "I was tired of fighting with them all the time, it was exhausting."

At one point, Ann Farino told her surviving daughter that "at least she died a virgin," when speaking of Carol. Cynthia found that both strange and a warning to her to enjoy life to the fullest.

"That was always in the back of my mind," Cynthia added. "That I would not let that happen to me, I was going to go out and have some fun and get a little wild and crazy."

"I wished that Carol had screwed the football team and enjoyed it," Cynthia said. "Who would have cared if she had been a slut? They were probably more embarrassed by her murder because it included a sexual overtone."

It was the late 1960s and early 1970s with the sexual revolution, hair and clothing style changes, drug use, and experimental music. But when it came to boys and sex, Cynthia stopped short, not wanting to do anything that would spark further parental confrontations.

"I never did anything when I was in Maplewood. I didn't want everybody to know what I was doing. Everybody knew who I was so anytime I did something everyone knew," she said. As for boys eager to lose their virginity, "I didn't want anyone practicing on me."

Cynthia recalled being drunk at a party in high school and someone saw her, one of Carol's friends who found Cynthia the next day and lectured her. "I couldn't do anything."

There was one other high school party Cynthia remembered in South Orange at a friend's house. That's where she met Tommy Langdon, a 20-year-old from Manhattan.

"I met him at a party that a girl in my class gave and I started dating him immediately after the party," she said. Despite his age, her parents allowed him to stay at their house after dates and train back to New York in the morning.

"I think they were glad they could monitor everything and maybe marry me off," Cynthia remembers. "My father kept saying, 'When are you leaving?' They kept hinting that they would approve of me marrying at a young age if it was someone they approved of."

Tommy had similar ideas and proposed to Cynthia at the prom her senior year, complete with a kneel-down and diamond ring. "I was mortified, it was embarrassing," she remembers. "I wanted to dig a hole and jump in."

"I told him I didn't want to get married and he got mad and I gave him the ring back. It fizzled out and we broke up," she said. "He called years later, but I was with my first husband."

She did not give up her virginity to Tommy either. "I realized that I wasn't attracted to him, I don't know why I went out with him for so long. He was probably seeing other women anyway."

Cynthia Farino sat still on the bleachers inside the gymnasium of Clinton Elementary School on the rainy afternoon of June 24, 1972. The red brick building that housed kindergarten through sixth graders was not supposed to be the site of the Columbia High School graduation that year.

But after two straight days of rain postponed the planned ceremony at Underhill Sports Complex, where the CHS football field is located, district administrators decided to simply move it indoors and hold the event that way.

The rushed gathering was so poorly planned and communicated to parents in the pre-Internet, non-email days that many parents thought they were not allowed to attend, according to a *News-Record* account. Rumors had been flying that the smaller school meant limited space.

"It was raining and usually they had it outside so they had it in the gym," Cynthia recalls. "And we were all sitting in the gym, it was nasty that day." She said no one marched up to a podium or even received their diplomas, which

Cynthia Farino, 1970s

were later sent in the mail: "We just stood up when our names were called."

The graduation debacle ended up drawing dozens of parents and students to a school board meeting the following week to complain about the lack of planning. It was later revealed that Seton Hall University had been available and school officials declined the offer. It was unclear why the event was not held inside the CHS gymnasium.

Among the absent parents were Frank and Ann Farino. Cynthia contends they knew about it but chose not to attend.

"Everybody else's parents went, but not my mother and father, they never went to anything," Cynthia said. "They did not go to my junior high school graduation, they never did anything or talk to my counselors or teachers about anything."

After the ceremony, Cynthia, Angela, and Gabe went shopping at the Livingston Mall. No gifts, grad parties, or Jersey Shore morning-after drives.

Cynthia recalls her parents' lack of interest in her grades or post-high school plans, even avoiding her guidance counselor or discussion of college during that senior year. It seemed they wanted to forget about Cynthia because she reminded them of Carol.

"I don't even remember who my counselor was, but my parents were trying to discourage me, they didn't want to pay for college," Cynthia remembered. "If I had gone to my guidance counselor and said I wanted to go to college I probably could have figured out a way, but I just did not think it was a possibility for me. None of my friends were going."

But, she adds, "I wanted to go to college, I wanted to do something, I didn't want to be a secretary. I hated it. I didn't know what I wanted to do, I had no dreams or goals, I was in survival mode, just getting through the day."

After graduation, Cynthia worked for weeks at the Maplewood Theater and saved enough for a trip to Freeport in the Bahamas with two friends. The threesome hit the island with money in hand and a need to cut loose for a while, she said.

"It was like a free-for-all. We weren't prepared," she said about the onslaught of single older men waiting to pounce. "One night we took a cab to another casino and this guy took off with my friend in the car. I had to run after the cab and screamed at the driver to stop. He did and let her out. What could have happened to us, we had no idea until we got there. It could have been anybody."

Then Cynthia met Dennis, a handsome, older blackjack dealer from England who approached her in a club and swept her off her feet.

"It wasn't my intention, we were just glad to get away and have some fun. I met him the first or second night in a club," she said about the after-hours spot where the dealers and casino workers would party into the morning. "He came over to us because his friend was talking to my friend."

Eventually, she was smitten by this suave older man and they stayed up all night dancing, drinking, and talking: "We went to this bar that was really pretty, out on the water and watched the sun come up."

The couple went their separate ways to sleep it off during the day. But the next night they found each other again, and again, and again.

"I would meet him each night after he got off work, 11:30 or 12 or 1 depending on how crowded the casino was," Cynthia said. "I practically moved in with him when I was there. I was only 17 and he thought I was 19, it was probably illegal. He had no idea how young I was."

But the romance continued for most of their 10-day stay, becoming intimate after just a few days, she said. "The first or second night, he was British, he was smooth and gorgeous," Cynthia remembered. "He was not American, not too young, he was a grown man. He was in his late 30's. He knew what he was doing."

Cynthia did not want to leave, especially to return to such a depressing and dysfunctional home life. Her friends had not seen her for a few days and when the time to leave arrived, they were not sure she was going to make it.

"On the last day they had to pack all of my clothes for me, I was not looking forward to leaving," she said. As for Dennis? "He called me at home a year later. I said, 'Who is this?' He was in New York. But I was already with someone else."

So the girls survived and headed home. For Cynthia, the past was still with her as her plane landed back at Newark Airport and she returned to the house on Orchard Street.

Little had changed with her parents, with her future, and most of all with why her sister had been killed.

Chapter Nine

As the 1960s drew to a close, Maplewood Police remained dumbfounded in their search for Carol's killer. After more than four years, they were no closer to a suspect, and seemed to have lost any trace of a stranger who might have come across Carol at Milt's Cup & Saucer or elsewhere.

Maplewood Police Chief William Peto, who had brought in hypnotists and psychics, and vowed years earlier to listen to anyone with a "shred of evidence," was nowhere close to solving the crime.

Police told the *Newark Evening News* in a 1967 story that they had been receiving about two tips a week, ranging from investigators in other New Jersey counties to cranks calling on the phone. "We've even received anonymous letters," one Maplewood police lieutenant told the newspaper. "But all have led up blind alleys."

Cops had also reviewed military records and questioned any local residents who entered the service in the months after the killing, perhaps as a way to escape scrutiny. Given that it was near the height of the Vietnam War, that was a major undertaking.

Peto had looked beyond Maplewood for similar crime sprees in other parts of New Jersey, and even elsewhere in the United States.

Then one day in 1969, the chief read about a string of young girl murders in Michigan that had begun in 1967 and seemed to mirror Carol's killing in many ways.

Later dubbed "The Michigan Murders," the string of killings "were savage, involving rape, strangulation, stabbing, or beating," according to *The Detroit News*, which said they began in July 1967 when 19-year-old East Michigan University student Mary Terese Fleszar was last seen alive on the evening of July 9, 1967, near her Ypsilanti, Michigan, apartment.

Her nude body was found by two teen boys nearly a month later stabbed multiple times and with her ankles and several fingers severed. She had also been beaten and raped, police revealed.

That first killing got pushed aside by much of the local media because it occurred two weeks before the deadly Detroit riots of 1967. That violent uprising, sparked by a routine police raid of an after-hours drinking spot, went on for five days of fires, beatings, and deaths, according to the *Detroit Free Press*.

In the end, 43 people were dead, 1,100 injured, and hundreds of stores looted and burned. There were also more than 7,200 arrests and 2,000 buildings destroyed.

"That first murder was put far off the front page because the riots broke out," recalls Greg Fournier, a former Ypsilanti resident and author of *Terror in Ypsilanti*. "People forgot about it for a while."

But it gained attention again nearly a year later, when another EMU student, Joan Schell, disappeared after hitchhiking in front of the student union in June 1968. Her body showed up with many stab wounds a week later in Ann Arbor, the *News* reported.

A year after that, between March and July 1969, five more young girls went missing, then later turned up dead. Among them were two teenage girls, two University of Michigan students, and another EMU student. Investigators also suspected there might have been a connection to a girl murdered in California.

"There was no motive for the murders and no suspects," states Edward Keyes' 1976 book, *The Michigan Murders*, a novelized account of the killings. "The women didn't know each other, didn't live high-risk lifestyles, and were seemingly selected by the killer at random."

Keyes added that "bright, ambitious and pretty young women, many only teenagers, were disappearing from sidewalks, footpaths, student centers, parties, and dances, only to turn up days or weeks later, the victims of unimaginable violence."

That seemed to fit Carol Ann Farino's murder perfectly, even if they had occurred more than 600 miles away.

Fournier said Ypsilanti, the small town on the outskirts of Ann Arbor—home of the University of Michigan—was struck especially hard after the fourth killing.

That was the brutal death of 13-year-old Dawn Basom, who was found on April 15, 1969, naked and beaten on the side of the road. Fournier said it put many people on high alert because she was the youngest victim and so savagely attacked.

"That one of the murders sent the community into anaphylactic shock, nobody seemed to trust anybody else," Fournier said in an interview. "Kids were not allowed to go play with their friends, it hit like a tidal wave, terribly hard. She was the fourth one and it really sent shockwaves through the entire state."

He said his later reporting found that "a lot of women would say how their parents forbade them from going outside, from dating, that was the biggest impression it made on women in particular."

Then there was Elaine Milliken, the daughter of then-Governor William Milliken. She was studying at the University of Michigan Law School at the time, and that sparked worry for the popular centrist governor as a concerned parent and gave the story statewide play, Fournier said.

"He was tuned into it and he became part of the story as well," Fournier said. At one point, Milliken used executive power to put the murders under the jurisdiction of the Michigan State Police, a move that angered some local law enforcement officials who saw it as a sign of criticism and disrespect.

The killings may have affected Elaine Milliken's career choices as she went on to become a respected attorney for civil rights and women's causes, helping to update state laws with stronger punishments for offenders and more protection for women during rape prosecutions.

Elaine went on to become a public defender in Detroit and later a legal consultant in Vermont. She died of cancer at age 45.

Fournier said the murders were so different—one a bludgeoned killing, another victim hit with a tree limb—that police had trouble finding a motive or routine. "He was trying a little bit of everything," Fournier said of the killer. "They were all so different."

Still, two of the 1969 Michigan killings caught Police Chief Peto's eye for similarities to Carol's murder in the cause of death: strangulation with a personal object belonging to the victim.

Jane Louise Mixer, who disappeared after posting a note on a college bulletin board seeking a lift across the state to her hometown of Muskegon, was found the morning after on a grave in a cemetery.

An autopsy revealed she'd been shot twice in the head with a .22-caliber pistol, then strangled with a stocking.

Four days after Mixer's body was found, on March 25, a surveyor discovered the nude, mutilated body of 16-year-old Maralynn Skelton, who had gone missing while hitch-hiking in Ann Arbor, according to *True Crime: Michigan: The State's Most Notorious Criminal Cases* by Tobin Buhke.

She had been beaten with a leather belt and found with a garter belt tied around her neck.

The first victim, Mary Fleszar, had been approached by a man seeking to lure her into his car, also reminiscent of Carol's likely attacker. Fournier wrote that Mary had left her off-campus apartment near Eastern Michigan University on the evening of July 9, a Sunday, to "get some fresh air."

"The July heat and humidity were oppressive, so she dressed lightly in a summer dress," Fournier wrote. "She was wearing a pair of woven toe sandals. Mary was not somebody who particularly liked walking, but she headed down the street alone that night."

About a half-hour into her walk, several witnesses saw a young man pull up next to her in a blueish-gray, two-toned car and offer a ride.

One of them told police, "Mary shook her head no and continued walking. The driver then sped around the block and pulled up aggressively into a driveway blocking her way on the sidewalk," according to Fournier. "Mary once again shook off his advances and walked around the car. Frustrated, the unidentified driver backed out onto the street and sped away screeching his tires."

That was the last time Mary was seen alive.

The scene was eerily similar to the confrontation Carol Ann Farino had with a pushy man in a car who pulled over to her days before her murder and offered a ride, according to Carol's friend, Gail Gawlick, who told police at the time that when she rebuffed him, he said he would "catch up to her later."

These facts were similar enough to spark Peto to send a letter to Michigan State Police on Aug. 11, 1969, seeking help with Carol's case.

"Due to the recent homicides in your state, certain similarities have been mentioned in the newspaper to warrant us to share information that may or may not be beneficial to both of our departments," the letter stated.

Peto then went on to describe the details of Carol's death, noting "it appeared that the victim had been handled very gently and that her body had been placed carefully on the ground."

Local police eventually arrested and convicted John Norman Collins, a Michigan man, for one of the killings: the murder of EMU student Karen Sue Beineman, 18, of Grand Rapids. She went missing and was found days later strangled and beaten.

Collins was sentenced to life in prison in 1970. But the other murders essentially remain unsolved, although many investigators believe Collins is responsible for at least some of them.

"In 1970, the *Detroit Free Press* reported the cases were 'all but officially closed in the minds of police officers close to the investigation,' and 'though law enforcement officials will not admit it publicly,' police agree Collins 'is the only possible suspect,'" according to a 2019 *Free Press* retrospective.

The newspaper stated that there had been a new effort to tie DNA to Collins or other suspects from the other young girl murders, but had no new information.

Fournier found no ties that would have put Collins in New Jersey in late 1966 when Carol Ann Farino was killed. But that does not mean the other murders might not have a connection to her, since Collins has so far been only convicted of one.

He said Collins had spent time in Boston in the late 1960s in between college stints. "He was accused and investigated for more than 17 murders and there were a pair of girls in the Boston area murdered and police had established he had been visiting Boston."

But no action was taken against Collins for the Boston killings, which included the bludgeoning to death of a Harvard University graduate student in early 1969. That crime was eventually solved in 2018 when DNA tied the case to a serial rapist who had been convicted of five other violent sex crimes and had died in 2001.

Chief Peto's outreach to Michigan was a clear indication of his desperation, and that of the police department, to find some links to the killer of Carol Ann Farino. But it's unclear what other trails he followed.

By 1969, there were several similar cases closer to home. Among them were the murders allegedly done by Robert Zarinsky of Linden, N.J., located just 10 miles south of Maplewood. He was a suspect in as many as six murders of young women between 1968 and 1974.

A *Star-Ledger* story on his 2008 death described him as "a savage predator, a short but powerfully built weightlifter whose alleged victims were beaten and garroted," later adding that his "long criminal history began with a series of petty crimes that quickly grew in seriousness when he was a teenager."

Born in 1940, Zarinksy would have been 26 when Carol was killed and would later be accused of several similar murders during the years that followed. But like Richard Cottingham, his deadly crimes were never brought to court until years later.

"Law enforcement authorities who pursued cases against him over the years said his signature included tempting girls into his car," *The Star-Ledger* reported, citing a practice likely used to abduct Carol. "One of them was Rosemary Calandriello of Atlantic Highlands. Zarinsky was convicted in 1975 of killing the timid 17-year-old who had disappeared on August 25, 1969, on her way to the corner store to buy a carton of milk. She was last seen alive in Zarinsky's Ford convertible, but her body has never been found."

That conviction, which would send Zarinsky away to prison until his 2008 death, was the first such guilty verdict in New Jersey against a killer involving a victim whose body was never found.

Zarinsky was also the prime suspect in the killings of Linda Balabanow of Union, N.J., in 1969, and Doreen Carlucci and Joanne Delardo of Woodbridge, N.J., in 1974. Investigators later said they lacked enough evidence to tie him to those cases.

He was also tried in 2001 for the shooting murder of Rahway police officer Charles Bernoskie during a 1958 burglary, but was acquitted.

In March 2008, just months before his death, Zarinsky pleaded not guilty to killing Jane Durrua, a 13-year-old East Keansburg girl who disappeared while walking home from her sister's house on November 4, 1968 (another similarity to Carol's disappearance almost two years to the day after she died).

Police had planned to use DNA taken from the suspect to tie him to Durrua's murder, but he died before the case went to trial.

Both *The Star-Ledger* and The *Asbury Park Press* have dubbed Zarinsky among New Jersey's "most notorious" killers.

"Robert Zarinsky's crime spree began in his native town of Linden when he vandalized two Jewish cemeteries and set five lumber yards on fire," the *Press* wrote in 2018. "His actions landed him a 13-month stay at the Trenton Psychiatric Hospital for evaluation. After his release, Zarinsky opened a small produce store with his father in his hometown."

He was also accused of kidnapping and raping 15-year-old Sharon Kennedy in 1961, but no charges were filed. The victim did not report the crime until years later when the statute of limitations had run out, police said.

The missing girl cases began in 1969 when young girls began disappearing near the Zarinsky family store. Calandriello went missing in August 1969 after witnesses spotted her in Zarinsky's car.

He was initially arrested and charged with kidnapping, but the charges were dropped. He would not be convicted of her murder until six years later.

"Authorities suspect there had been more victims through the years," *The Star-Ledger* reported at the time of his 2008 death. "Zarinsky himself often hinted as much. He once wrote in a letter to *The Star-Ledger*, 'There is so much I could tell you about, going back to the year 1956.'"

But even as he allegedly stalked and killed young women in the late 1960s, Zarinsky maintained a sense of normalcy. In 1967 he married 17-year-old Florence Lynn McDermott of Cliffwood Beach, six months after she gave birth to their son, also named Robert. But the child died of asthma-related issues in July 1968, a month short of his second birthday.

Less than six months later, Jane Durrua disappeared on her way home from an older sister's house. Her body was discovered the next morning in a field by railroad tracks where she often walked.

Just a few months after that, on March 26, 1969, Linda Balabanow was seen leaving her job at a Roselle, N.J., drug store. A month later, her bloated body, beaten with a chain, was discovered in a section of the Raritan River in Woodbridge. She had been beaten and cut up with electrical wire.

Calandriello went missing four months later.

One might speculate that the death of Zarinsky's son prompted his rage, depression, or some combination of both that might have set him off.

In December 1974, a few months before Zarinsky's trial for the death of Calandriello, two more girls disappeared—Delardo, 15, and Carlucci, 14—who had attended a church event near their homes in Colonia, N.J. Their bludgeoned bodies were found two weeks later on a path in Manalapan in Monmouth County.

Zarinsky was also ordered to take a DNA test to see if he had any links to a 1973 murder of Ann Logan, 19, a student at Seton Hall University who was beaten to death after leaving her job at a convenience store. Seton Hall is located in South Orange, right next to Maplewood.

"Logan's body was discovered in a vacant lot in Roselle, within walking distance of Zarinsky's home in Linden," *NJ.com* stated. "The killing bore striking similarities to the others for which Zarinsky was a suspect, but his DNA didn't match, confounding Union County prosecutors who still consider Zarinsky her killer."

As with Richard Cottingham, Robert Zarinsky could also be investigated for Carol's murder due to time and detail similarities. But as Maplewood Police Detective Christopher Dolias said, police found no direct links so they dropped Cottingham as a potential suspect. It is unknown if Zarinsky even crossed their radar.

There also remains a handful of unsolved murders in Northern New Jersey involving young, dark-hard women who were violently killed in ways similar to Carol's death. One of those responsible may well have ended Carol's life, too.

The first victim was Alys Jean Everhardt, 18, of Fair Lawn, N.J., who was found stabbed to death in her upscale suburban home on September 24, 1965. Her father discovered her body when he returned home from work.

Alys had been stabbed multiple times and her clothes had been partially removed, according to *The Morning Call* of Paterson. A nursing student, Alys had left school for the day and was waiting to leave with her father for a family funeral. Among those questioned was her boyfriend, but police never made any arrests.

Three years later, on Aug. 31, 1968, Joan Carole Freeman, 22, of West Paterson, was found with her throat slashed and her skull crushed in an office where she worked in Clifton, according to *The Courier-Post* of Camden. A pretty, single secretary at the pharmaceutical firm of Hoffman-La Roche, Inc., she was found "sprawled on the floor," according to the news account.

Her body was discovered on the second floor of Building 34 in the 86-building giant drug-making campus. A funeral home director who oversaw her memorial described it as a "crime of extreme brutality." Cops did not say at the time if she had been sexually assaulted.

A former high school cheerleader and decent student, she was described by her brother as someone who might have been too friendly to strangers, not unlike Carol Ann Farino, who likely let her kindness open the door to a killer.

It was later determined by police that Freeman was attacked from behind, struck in the back of the head with a wooden mallet later found nearby. She was found by a guard making late safety checks.

Police made the case a major cause, due in part to heavy media publicity and the notice the case received because of the location in a well-known, international corporate headquarters.

Investigators reportedly interviewed and/or did background checks on more than 300 people, including the guards who had been on duty and nearly all employees who were on the job that day. Many also took lie-detector tests.

Detectives dug into the Freeman murder for more than a year afterward, including empaneling a Passaic County grand jury. But the case remains unsolved. Some even claim her ghost is haunting the Hoffman-La Roche offices where she was found.

Less than a year later, Gilda Ryan, 34, was found stabbed to death in her Sayreville home, about 15 miles south of Maplewood. A bit older than the others, the mother of three fit a similar look, with short black hair and a youthful smile.

On April 29, 1969, her live-in boyfriend, Robert Lewis, discovered her body early in the morning, a brutal bloody scene after she had been stabbed 13 times, according to Middlesex County's Crimestoppers program website. A kitchen knife, believed to be the murder weapon, was found at the scene of the murder, investigators said.

Then there's Susan Davis and Elizabeth Perry, both 19, who were found murdered in woods near the Garden State Parkway in South Jersey on Memorial Day weekend, 1969.

The co-eds had been vacationing at a house in Ocean City on the Jersey Shore and were driving back to Davis's Pennsylvania home early that morning. They had stopped off in Somers Point, N.J., to eat an early breakfast, according to *The Record* of Bergen County, and were found stabbed to death an hour later.

Numerous theories have followed the killings, which also included the suspension of a state trooper for failing to follow protocol when he found their abandoned car. Trooper John L. Sterr was suspended for two weeks, but he and his lawyer claimed he was scapegoated because of the attention given to the case that remained unsolved.

Patrick T. McGahn, Sterr's attorney, said during a hearing that claims against his client were "absolutely, totally erroneous," according to *The Central Home News* of New Brunswick.

Investigators later tried to tie the killings to the Michigan murders, according to news reports. That may have been what tipped Chief Peto to those killings, but no link was ever made.

Finally, a psychologist who had interviewed notorious serial killer Ted Bundy claimed that he was linked to the Davis and Perry murders, according to a 1989 *Asbury Park Press* story after Bundy's death that year.

Arthur Norman, who had interviewed Bundy as part of the psychiatric review of his case in 1987, said Bundy had details on the killings, but Norman offered few specifics. Norman said Bundy had provided him with "amazing…details" of the case, but no outright confession.

Investigators said they took the information seriously because Bundy had attended Temple University in nearby Philadelphia in 1969. Years later, Bundy biographer Richard Larsen, a friend of Perry's mother, said he believed Bundy had also been connected to the crimes. He claimed Bundy had confessed to him of murders at the Jersey Shore that year but did not mention them specifically.

The murders remain unsolved.

There's no indication that Chief Peto or Maplewood Police reached out to any of these jurisdictions or sought to look into the murders or Zarinsky as a possible suspect despite the timing of the other murders, the similarity in the victims, and the proximity of location.

And even today the Maplewood Police indicate no DNA samples from Carol's clothing or personal items found with her have ever been tested or run through the New Jersey DNA database.

"The last time this was really looked into, DNA wasn't a prominent thing, so it wasn't sent out," Detective Dolias told me, citing a brief 2005 re-opening of the case. "We will see if there is anything we can send off to a lab for the state or a private lab for DNA. Even now we might have a problem with a state-run lab, they are so backlogged. When we have stuff sent out it takes a long time to come back."

Backlogs did not seem to stop investigators in several of the murders involving Richard Cottingham or Robert Zarinsky that were solved in recent years. As I have stated earlier, both men were tied to decades-old murders in recent years via DNA.

But since Maplewood police have not done such testing and refuse to disclose most of what their 54-year long investigation has included, we may never know.

Chapter Ten

After a fun, adventurous, and romantic whirlwind in the Bahamas, Cynthia returned to the same Maplewood she had left behind in August 1972, with no excitement or hope about what would come next.

The trauma of the past years and the unsolved murder of her sister weighing on her almost daily would affect her future relationships, career decisions, and emotional well-being for the next few decades.

Cynthia would fall into a marriage that was a mistake, jobs she hated, and eventually an ongoing love affair that would break her heart and shatter her views of what real love and commitment could mean.

Meanwhile, her parents' lack of compassion and guidance during her teen years permeated her entry into adulthood, leaving her with little focus and few options to pursue what would make her happy.

Along the way, there was the memory and image of Carol—her older sister's bright smile, beautiful presence, and loving support, someone taken away too soon.

"I always thought about her around the holidays, how different my life would have been," Cynthia laments. "She would have been married and had children. She would have had a nice family and would have been a good mother. I would have been a totally different person if this did not happen. I changed drastically because of this. My parents were horrible after it happened."

Cynthia also continued to be haunted by the mystery: Who killed her and why? Living in Maplewood and nearby for the next few years only deepened that pressure and anger as Maplewood Police never contacted the family with any hope or updates. The Farinos eventually wanted nothing to do with a police force they believed mishandled the facts and sought to pin it on Cynthia and Carol's father.

"I never heard from the police, not a word," Cynthia recalls angrily. "They never contacted us about anything, like it was not going on at all. Like there was no investigation."

Cynthia wanted to go to college after returning from the glorious trip to the Bahamas, or at least do something interesting and exciting. But Ann and Frank remained adamant that no money was available and would actively dissuade her with claims she was not smart enough or able to keep it up for four years.

That led to her enrollment at Berkeley Secretarial School in East Orange. An ad from that time declared that "Berkeley Girls are special!" It later boasted: "Berkeley's 1- or 2-year programs are designed to develop your extra-special secretarial qualities."

Cynthia did not agree and went into it kicking and screaming.

"My sister was going to go there so I had to go there, and I bet she wouldn't have liked it either," she recalls. "They were so worried about us not being able to get jobs, that was their whole focus."

But Cynthia wanted more. She had just escaped from high school and had a wondrous summer of love, travel, and parties and saw the world as a wide-open place.

Being back home only reminded her of the sad situation around her house as her parents remained stuck in anger and guilt-ridden depression. There was also a constant reminder of Carol's death. Despite the change in home address, still living in Maplewood and hearing nothing from police about the investigation kept the tragedy alive and without closure.

Ann and Frank also never raised the issue with Cynthia, which frustrated her further because she was still seeking answers.

"They would talk about it, but with each other and when they thought

I wasn't listening, that's how I found out most of the information about her," she said. "They always talked about her when I wasn't around, frustration over not finding anything. My mother would say they probably still thought they had something to do with it and they stopped talking to the police because they were trying to pin it on my father."

Cynthia never visited Carol's grave in those days: Plot 51 in Section 32, Block B, Tier H at the Gate of Heaven Cemetery in East Hanover, N.J.—some 10 miles west of Maplewood.

She had been barred from the graveside ceremony after her sister's funeral and had no interest in seeing it during those frustrating, lonely times.

"I never went to the grave, I don't know why," she said, noting she finally saw it in 2015 after Ann's funeral and burial in the same North Jersey cemetery. "I never went to the grave because my parents would go without me. I wouldn't have wanted to go with them, I didn't."

Cynthia said she still had a bad relationship with Frank and even harbored doubts about his innocence for years after the murder. She had no interest in going to the grave with him but was also not in a rush to go alone: "I didn't have a good relationship with him or with my mother, I was angry with her that she put up with him."

Still, Carol's memory remained in Cynthia's daily life, especially when she was reminded of her favorite things—food, clothes, or sisterly talks.

"It was always on my mind, I always thought about her every day of my life, something or other would make me think of her," Cynthia said. "Just being in Maplewood made me think of her and how I hated the cops."

Then there was Carol's favorite song: "In the Still of the Night," recorded by several groups in the 1950s and 1960s. The song's lyrics were eerily appropriate for Carol's tragic death:

"In the still of the night, I held you.
Held you tight.
'Cause I love,
Love you so.
Promise I'll never
Let you go."

"If I heard that song," Cynthia said. "It took me back to hearing her play it in her room." She also dreamed about her departed sister often, "Quite a bit."

With all of those demons, feelings, and memories, Cynthia dutifully enrolled at Berkeley Secretarial School in the fall of 1972, signing up for the required shorthand, typing, and limited accounting.

"The shorthand, I couldn't stand it, it was so boring," she remembers. "It was all memorization, squiggly lines that mean something, it was annoying. Very little deviation and the whole outside world was another world I wanted to see. "

Each day that fall was a boring routine with no creative outlet or interesting goals. Her parents or a neighbor would drive her to the Maplewood rail station and she'd grab a morning train to East Orange, just a 15-minute jaunt east.

"I didn't want to do it, I wanted to have fun," she said, admitting, "my typing wasn't bad, but I think they wanted me to type more without any mistakes but I was not into it."

That did not sit well with Ann and Frank, who demanded improvement in typing and even forced her to purchase an expensive business-level IBM typewriter with her own funds.

"After a while, I hated it so much I would take the train to East Orange and meet a friend and we would take the bus to New York City and hang out there all day," Cynthia said. "Or we went to Newark and went shopping at Bamberger's and hang around and stuff."

By the spring 1973 semester, Cynthia had had it and dropped out, deciding that working and making money instead of spending it on office equipment for a job she never wanted was a better plan: "I finally told my parents I wasn't going to go back and that was a major ordeal. I didn't have a car so any job I got I would have to walk to."

She soon joined Liberty Mutual Insurance, also in East Orange, in a clerical position for the claims adjusters' office. Since she had the travel by rail down pat, each day's transportation was easy. And at least it brought in money rather than having to spend it on needless tuition, in her mind.

That's also where Cynthia met Nick, a handsome claims adjuster some eight years older than her. He pursued her for about nine months and several colleagues warned both of them not to get involved.

"He kept asking me out and he was too old for me. He kept asking and he finally wore me down," she recalled. "The other guys kept telling him I was too young for him. He was also a divorced man and I thought, 'I am only 18.'"

But she also saw Nick as a way out and someone exciting and willing to do what he wanted, something Cynthia learned to appreciate.

"He had a motorcycle and we used to take the motorcycle down to Matawan," she said about the Jersey Shore town where Nick's family-owned The White Shanty, a local tavern and restaurant. "His brother ran it full-time with his mother and Nick would go down on the weekends and help out."

As the romance blossomed, Cynthia left the insurance job and signed on with a realtor in South Orange, a closer location and slightly different job as a receptionist who also answered phones: "It was really boring and I didn't like that."

She soon moved down the street to a finance company and became something of a collector of loans from deadbeats: "I worked the phones all day and people would fall behind on their loans and you had to call them and get them to pay."

The job was a bit different and opened her eyes to what a lot of married men were like: cheaters who hid money problems from their wives. She discovered that many of the deadbeats were having affairs or, at the very least, keeping their financial problems from their spouses.

She said many of the clients gave specific instructions not to call them at home, offering work numbers or sometimes their mistresses' home phone.

"You couldn't call them at home because their wives didn't know about the loan. They took out loans to give to the mistresses or they would spend it on things that their wife didn't know about," Cynthia explained. "A lot of the men had loans for the women on the side, that really was enlightening. But I didn't like the people I worked with."

After a few months, Cynthia and Nick were a regular item, but she soured on most of the jobs she had and would quit or just not show up.

"I would quit jobs and just go on vacation, my parents were livid," she remembers. "The finance company fired me after I made clear I did not like the job. I went on and off unemployment a few times and worked a little bit, but that's it."

By 1976, the table was set for marriage. But even that seemed doomed given Nick's lackluster proposal. He offered no engagement ring and failed to even get down on one knee or actually "pop" the question.

"He said, 'when do you want to get married?'" Cynthia recalled, noting it took place in a South Orange Chinese restaurant, hardly a bastion of romance. "He was so sure I would say yes."

She believes part of her willingness to tie the knot was a desperate need to get away from Ann and Frank, who grew angrier and more depressed than ever as the police dragged their feet on Carol's murder. Her parents also felt that Frank remained an unspoken suspect.

"I think I did want to get away," Cynthia said. "I wasn't madly in love with him, I wasn't in a hurry to get married. Nick wasn't very demonstrative or affectionate, he wasn't very interested in sex and he wasn't very good at it. He didn't seem to be interested."

As for her parents: "They were pushing me out the door, they were ready to get rid of me because I wasn't doing what they wanted me to, I did not behave the way they wanted, but that was their fault."

The wedding was set for November 16, 1976, just two weeks after the 10th anniversary of Carol's murder.

But the planning was its own torment, too, Cynthia said. That should have tipped her off as well that it might be a bad idea.

First, they could not get married in a Catholic church because of Nick's divorced status. But when they found a small Methodist church on Boyden Avenue in Maplewood, Cynthia liked it more: "I liked the church, and the minister there was great."

The church was later torn down for apartments.

When Ann and Frank started overseeing the planning, it went downhill: "They were horrible, I couldn't pick anything. My mother took over everything. I couldn't pick out my dress, I hated my dress. She was horrible. She would make me think I was fat. I didn't get to pick anything except the colors. I could have looked a lot better if I had worn what I wanted."

Angela was her maid of honor and Gabe took a bridesmaid's post, with most of her extended family in attendance, but no children allowed: "It was a big wedding." The reception was in a West Orange hotel.

It was also another reminder of Carol, who was clearly in Cynthia's thoughts and likely would have been a bridesmaid or maid of honor had she lived. She said her parents forbid her from offering any kind of remembrance or prayer for her missing sister during the ceremony.

"It was embarrassing to the family I think, the rest of my family, they just wanted to sweep it under the rug," she said of Carol's death even 10 years later. "I always thought about that because I know it would have been different. I knew my life would have been different if she had been there."

At one point, as Cynthia waited for the nuptials to begin, she became so nervous and tense that a friend offered her a puff of marijuana before she went down the aisle. "I started giggling, people thought it was nerves, but I was high," she said later. "After the wedding, I was laughing and I was high. Nick thought that was funny."

The newlyweds set up house in an attic apartment of a Victorian home in Montclair, about 10 minutes north of Maplewood. It offered no washer or dryer and a third-story walk-up that kept the young couple in shape.

Nick remained at the same insurance company where they had met and Cynthia tried her hand at other jobs, but few would take. Nick spent more time in Matawan at The White Shanty on weekends and Cynthia would often go with him.

They eventually moved to a bigger apartment in neighboring Union County in 1977. Soon after, Nick's brother who had helped run the bar/restaurant with his mother in Matawan sold the place and moved to Kansas City, opening a hardware store there and urging Nick and Cynthia to go west as well.

"We stayed here but Nick was thinking about it and talked on the phone and his brother kept wanting him to come out," she recalled. "They knew how to make money, I had to admire them for that. He was doing great and he kept saying to Nick to come out so he could expand."

By 1978, Nick and Cynthia relocated to the Midwest, landing in the Kansas City suburb of Grandview, Missouri. Nick joined the hardware store full time and Cynthia spent time there as an employee as well.

But it didn't last.

"I helped them with the business and when I was cashiering, his brother was very rude, he would fly off the handle," she remembered. "And I wouldn't put up with it and walked out one day. Who was he to yell at me? I walked out and never went back."

Cynthia soon sought another career in salon and cosmetology work, enrolling in a local beauty school and eventually getting a cosmetology license to work in that area. She wound up in Overland Park, Kansas, at a salon inside The Jones Store, a Macy's-like department story that had its own beauty parlors.

The money for the couple was fine, but the job eventually became dangerous for Cynthia, who suffered respiratory problems from dirty air vents over her salon space.

"The air conditioning vent and the heating vent for the salon blew right on my station," she said. "And they never cleaned anything so it got fungus."

She was finally diagnosed with Bronchopulmonary aspergillosis, along with the asthma she had since childhood. She remains on medication to this day.

"They didn't know what it was and they thought I had tuberculosis," she recalled. "I was miserable and once they figured it out I was okay." But she still had to leave and regrets not taking legal action.

"I tried to sue them, but no one in the salon would back me up so I got screwed," she said. "Nick would never take an interest in anything that would help me. He was always worried about work."

She recalls once getting pneumonia and having to go to the emergency room. But Nick made her wait several hours and sleep in the car until he would take her to the hospital: "That was the end of my marriage, I should have put a fork in it then."

Then Ann and Frank showed up.

They surprised Cynthia and Nick when they decided to move to Kansas City in 1980: "I couldn't get rid of them. They forced themselves on us. I knew they would expect to have Sunday dinner and all that, I was not into that. They came out for Christmas and wouldn't leave."

By 1982, Nick and Cynthia were further apart due to his long hours and her need for a connection that went beyond just cohabitation and paying the bills together.

She would soon find one in a blast from the past.

That year she went back to Maplewood for her 10-year high school reunion, joining Angela and Gabe for the festivities, but with Nick left behind to work.

The trio stayed at Angela's house in Millburn and enjoyed the gatherings as if no time had passed for them: "It was fun, we had such a good time. We had a blast and Gabe met her husband there."

Cynthia Farino, 1981

Cynthia met someone, too.

A former classmate named Daniel, a friendly, handsome fellow graduate she hardly remembered from past days.

As she and her friends caroused with others inside the Martinsville Inn about 10 miles west of Maplewood that night, Cynthia left thoughts of her other life behind and felt freer than she had in years.

The timing was perfect for Daniel to grab her attention.

"He just came up to me and asked if I remembered him and I didn't," Cynthia said. "He was over six feet tall. In high school, he looked like a little kid."

It didn't take long for things to progress. After the party, they went out to dinner and one thing led to another.

Soon they were together and spending the night as quick-found lovers, with Nick far from Cynthia's thoughts.

"That's where it started," Cynthia remembers somewhat sheepishly. "I had an affair with him on and off for years, he and I would get together and it was like dating when I went home."

When the reunion weekend was over, Cynthia did not want to return to her real life, but responsibilities demanded it. She flew back to Kansas City and never spoke of the weekend's events to Nick.

But they would not end.

"I kept it separate, I wasn't happily married and Nick was not the person for me," she admits. "That was one of the reasons I eventually left him."

But the couple stayed married for several years after the reunion as Cynthia flew back and forth to New Jersey regularly, often picking up with Daniel for short stints and long weekends.

"I was so busy and so crazy, I was pretty wild," she said. "I think it hit me when my mother said to me that at least (Carol) died a virgin, it was not going to be me. That added to my behavior. I got this attitude that I was going to raise hell and do what I want and that's what I did."

By the summer of 1984, Cynthia and Nick were essentially married on paper only. She remained a resident of Missouri but spent that entire summer in New Jersey. She stayed with Angela and saw Daniel regularly.

"We were in New York during the day and went to Long Beach Island and Pennsylvania," she recalls. "I wasn't planning to go back. I stayed with Angela, we were very close and like family. Daniel and I would go away on the weekends when he was off." They even took a trip to Cancun, Mexico, at one point.

"(Nick) was always working, I don't think it bothered him. I had done that before," Cynthia said about her New Jersey trips. "One summer I went home to have a procedure done on my face with this dermatologist. I would visit my parents and my aunts."

Cynthia eventually moved to New Jersey for good in October 1984, got an apartment on Rutgers Street in Maplewood, and started to attend a beauty school. She trained in New York City to get her certificate in esthetician training to allow her to do facials and massage. After three months, she graduated and was accredited.

"Daniel wanted me out here so I moved back for that. We were feeling it out," she said. "I was happy with him, but he could never make up his mind."

Daniel owned a home cleaning business and lived in his parents' Maplewood home after they died. He even rented out some of the rooms for extra cash.

Cynthia ended up working in a Lord and Taylor's salon in neighboring Millburn. As for Nick? "I am sure he suspected an (affair) and I don't think he cared," she said. "Daniel kind of romanced me, he made me think he was in love with me, but he could never firm it up and make a decision."

But being in New Jersey again meant constant reminders of Carol.

"I didn't like living in Maplewood because of that," she said. "I never wanted to be there, I only did it because I moved back for him. I should have moved to Millburn or something. I didn't hang out there that much, I never went to Maplewood Village and stayed away."

But Nick was not out of the picture. They remained married and he came to New Jersey in 1985 to win Cynthia back. Daniel had broken off with her and married someone else earlier that year.

"It was someone from high school he had been on and off with," she said. "But they lasted two weeks and then split up."

Still, Daniel's departure left her devastated, and quite vulnerable as her husband sought to revive their marriage.

By April 1985 Nick had convinced her to return to Missouri and give it another chance. She moved back and did not work at all for two years.

"I was devastated about Daniel, I could barely get out of bed. I never felt that way about anyone. I could barely function," she said.

By that time, Nick's hardware business had expanded to two stores and he was as busy as ever. Ann and Frank Farino, meanwhile, were still living in Missouri as well.

Cynthia returned to New Jersey again in 1986, visiting Angela and traveling into New York City. "When we were walking in Soho I heard someone whistle," she remembered. "I turned around and it was Daniel. I looked at him once and kept on walking."

When they returned to New Jersey, Daniel reached out and she agreed to see him. They met up later that day, spent the night together, and stayed together for a whole weekend: "He left and I stayed down the shore with my cousin and her children and never called him."

But Cynthia saw him again on that same trip, then she left for Missouri and would see him again. "When I came home I would see him, but I knew it would not last. I would kind of jerk him around to let him get a taste of his own medicine."

By this time her love life had become something of a ping-pong game, back and forth between two men and two relationships that were barely meeting her needs. If only her sister had been there to help her.

Then there was EST (Erhard Training Seminars), the international self-help events that first broke on to the scene in the 1970s and were still going in the mid-1980s when Cynthia hooked up with them.

Given all of the craziness in her life, a friend suggested she check out the unusual organization, so she looked into the Kansas City-area group.

"It is taking the reins of your life and stop making excuses and not blaming everything on other people," she recalled. "You either muddle through the best you can and don't leave it up to fate. Don't drift through your life and expect great things to happen."

Created by former salesman Werner Erhard, the sessions received both positive and negative responses in their heyday, with some claiming they amounted to abuse and others contending they were a miraculous answer to emotional issues.

Stories arose of hosts using profanity and calling members obscene names, while also barring them from bathroom breaks or enough food.

By the time Cynthia joined, however, the organization had been re-dubbed "The Forum," and took a more positive and helpful approach. She flew to St. Louis in late 1988 and attended two weekends of training, while still married to Nick.

"He was not interested at all, he thought it was crazy," she remembers. "Angela told me to do it, she had done it and thought it would help me. I trusted her enough and I still do. I knew it wasn't going to be some crazy thing if she did it."

She described it as a large group of people sharing their problems and lives and seeking positive solutions and a sense of camaraderie.

"They make you see that other people have the exact same problems, although nobody had a sister that was murdered," she said. "I wanted to get what I could get out of it. They told me that I was probably dragging my sister around on my back with me, which was true.

"That was the first time I was able to talk about Carol's death. I could never talk about it to my parents or my friends. When I got to the Forum, I just felt like I could talk about it."

"I always tried to accommodate my parents even though I didn't like them. I felt like I owed them something because Carol died, they made me feel like that."

She said the strange rules of the past, like no bathroom breaks, no longer existed: "They gave you breaks and the only thing you couldn't do was to drink, they asked you not to drink alcohol. I stayed in the hotel where they were doing it."

Cynthia said the Forum was a helpful, positive experience and she stayed with it for about a year, attending weekly meetings in Kansas City.

"They told me that I was one of those people who just about makes it, but I don't quite get there," she said. "I never attainted a level of where I thought I should have been."

But after a while, the experience became tiresome and she felt she had reached the best level she could. She also resented the growing demands to help recruit members and raise money.

"I had come for myself and that was annoying, I didn't have time for it," she said. "I was calling people and I didn't join for that. I joined for myself. It wasn't furthering my experience at all. But I felt better about things and was more able to stop with the 'poor me' stuff."

By 1987, Cynthia and Nick had separated and she was back on the dating market. She would soon meet another man.

But that relationship would end with distrust and murder.

Chapter Eleven

Just a few months after Cynthia Farino graduated from Columbia High School, two local girls mysteriously disappeared and were later found murdered with no immediate suspects.

Both victims resembled Carol's pretty appearance and dark hair, both were close to her in age, and both were believed to have been strangled, just like Carol. Each was also found dead in secluded off-road areas just a few miles from Maplewood. Police believe they were killed just weeks apart in 1972.

Eventually, they would also share the same suspect: Otto Neil Nilson.

Nilson, 37 at the time of the murders, was a Long Island native who had graduated from nearby Seton Hall University and served two years in the U.S. Army. He later married and had five children, settling in South Orange and working as an accountant in Maplewood—right across the street from Milt's Cup & Saucer.

But when Carol Ann Farino was killed in 1966, Nilson was not even known to the police. Married in 1959 to Carole S. Spangenberger, Nilson began working as an accountant in Maplewood Village soon after and would do so for the next 10 years.

With no clues pointing to him and no police record at the time of

Carol's death, Nilson was not even close to being a suspect then.

But six years later, his name would be among the most wanted in Maplewood and South Orange after two strangely similar killings that also mirrored Carol's slaying in many ways.

Jeannette DePalma, 16, was last seen alive leaving her home in Springfield, N.J.—just one town west of Maplewood—on Aug. 7, 1972. She was found six weeks later on a hilltop of the nearby Watchung Reservation, so decomposed that a cause of death was hard to establish but at one point was ruled to have been strangulation, just like Carol.

A week after Jeannette disappeared, 24-year-old Joan Kramer, a South Orange graduate student, was last seen getting into a car with a man along South Orange Avenue. About two weeks later, her body was found in a ditch along Elizabeth River Park in Union, N.J., also a neighboring town to Maplewood, according to a later *New York Times* report.

An autopsy found Joan had died of strangulation, while her shoes were missing, both similarities to Carol. Jeanette and Joan also resembled Carol as dark-haired, young beauties with reputations for being friendly and outgoing.

But their deaths had more intrigue and rumor surrounding them than Carol's killing. Both killings were chronicled in the 2015 book, *Death on the Devil's Teeth*, by Jesse P. Pollack and Mark Moran.

Pollack and Moran are better known as the creators and editors of *Weird NJ*, a magazine, series of books, and a website devoted to what it terms "New Jersey's local legends and best-kept secrets."

In the book, the authors seek to tie De Palma's and Kramer's murders together and give an overview of Nilson's suspected involvement in both. They also touch on Carol Ann Farino, but with little specificity or extended reporting.

The book's title comes from the location where De Palma's body was found, Devils Teeth, a high-ridge section of the Houdaille Quarry in Springfield. "That's what it was called back then," a Springfield firefighter told Pollack and Moran. "It was originally known as the Devil's Skull back in the 1920s."

The ridge also has long, narrow grooves in the side that resemble jagged long teeth or knives. Reports indicated De Palma's body was surrounded by rocks, especially her head, and an apparent cross, according to the book.

Other strange occurrences surrounded the disappearance and killing of DePalma. On the morning she went missing, it turned out that her cousin, Lisa, had been missing for a month, but Jeanette's parents did not tell her until that morning. Lisa was later found to have run away and returned unharmed, according to *Devil's Teeth*.

The book later revealed that one of the Springfield firefighters who assisted in removing Jeanette's body from the quarry was so shaken by the incident that he suffered emotional trauma for more than a year and finally killed himself in 1973. Don Stewart, a Vietnam veteran, "was surrounded by fellow Springfield firefighters and police officers, all begging him to drop his pistol," the book states, just before he shot himself in the heart.

It adds that Stewart's suicide began what some local firefighter and police department veterans dubbed "The DePalma Curse." The book claims that after DePalma's death, Fire Chief Robert Day suddenly retired and worked as a janitor, while another deputy chief, Ed Erskine, quit the department, divorced his wife, and ended up living in a car. Two other department veterans also reportedly quit without reason.

The strange location of where DePalma's body was found and the alleged circle of rocks and crosses, also prompted speculation about the occult and satanic worship. Rumors began to fly that she and/or her killer must have been involved in such worship or strange practices.

Kramer's death did not produce as many unusual connections. But shortly after her disappearance, a demand for ransom was received, according to reports at the time.

A member of a wealthier family than either Jeanette DePalma or Carol Ann Farino, Joan Kramer had grown up on upscale Crest Drive in the affluent Newstead neighborhood of South Orange.

Situated high above most of the village, the area boasts a classic mansion once owned by Joe DiMaggio and Marilyn Monroe, and numerous other millionaires' residences.

In 1972, Kramer's father, Julian, was the president of Suburban Foods, Inc. and the Tantleff Beef Company, both of Newark. Joan had attended the exclusive Kent Place School in Summit, N.J., and was a graduate student at Columbia University when she died.

The Tuesday night that she was last seen, the family was having a small summer party with some 30 guests, according to *Devil's Teeth*. Among those in attendance was Joan's boyfriend, Bernard Davidoff, another Columbia student. The couple had already been talking marriage.

But at one point during the gathering they had an argument, and Joan left and walked about a mile down the hill to the center of South Orange, finally ducking behind Gruning's Ice Cream parlor, the same spot where Carol Ann Farino's father had shown up looking for her the night she died.

In the alley, she found a payphone and called a friend in Manhattan to vent about the argument. Her friend told her to calm down and wait then catch a cab back home and try to patch things up.

Joan then phoned her parents and told them she was on a "deserted street in Newark" and would take a taxi home soon, but it's unclear why she lied. Pollack and Moran write that she turned left on South Orange Avenue and began walking toward the hill back to Crest Drive.

But instead of getting a cab, she was seen by witnesses approaching a car at South Orange Avenue and Sloan Street, just in front of a New Jersey Transit railroad bridge that led to the South Orange Station. After speaking to the unidentified driver through the driver's side window, she got in and they drove away, witnesses said.

She was last seen alive at just after midnight.

Two days later, the Kramers began to receive phone calls from a man demanding ransom. Given the family's wealth and community status, this was not entirely surprising.

The caller wanted $20,000 and the Kramers agreed. But when Julian Kramer twice dropped the money at a predetermined spot, it was not picked up.

The man called back and said he could not find it, then gave them one more chance to pay the ransom. He directed Julian Kramer to a phone booth across from Newark's Weequahic Park, according to *Devil's Teeth*. He left the money, which was taken soon after.

But the "kidnapper" turned out to be a fake and Joan Kramer was later found on Aug. 28, 1972, lying face down in the Union, N.J., park. Two people walking along a path discovered the body in the afternoon along with a pick-ax that police believed was used to try to bury her.

As South Orange police continued their investigation into the killing of Joan Kramer, they came across witnesses who claimed to have seen her get into the car on that last night. Among them, one witness believed she had enough information to give police a good description for an artist's sketch, which they used.

Eventually, the sketch was distributed to the press and ended up in every local newspaper. It was a frightening resemblance to Nilson's college photo—both offered a long, straight nose; large ears, and a somewhat receding dark hairline.

Among those who saw it was Curt Knoth, a neighbor of Otto Nilson who lived next door to him on Summit Avenue.

"When that witness sketch from the Kramer case appeared in the newspaper, everyone in South Orange knew right away it was Otto Nilson," Curt Knoth told the authors of *Devils Teeth*.

The Nilsons had been in South Orange for about 10 years when the Kramer and DePalma murders occurred, with a reputation as friendly, kind people. Otto's wife, Carole, was a full-time mother for their five children while Otto did well at the Maplewood accounting firm where he worked.

Neighbors found him kind and helpful. One local recalled Nilson's practice of pulling loose teeth out for children too afraid of doing it themselves. Others recalled his family barbecues that included many of the neighborhood residents. Knoth called him the "master of ceremonies" at his own outdoor parties.

But those who knew the Nilsons said things started to go downhill for the family by 1971. Knoth told Pollack and Moran that Otto and Carole began to drink, and "Otto went bad." He described the Nilson home as being neglected and "disgusting...dirty dishes out on the table forever... bad, it was gross."

He recalled a time when the children and their parents had to be "de-fleaed" with medical visits and special shampoos to remove the insect contamination. Another neighbor cited an incident at a neighborhood party when Otto got into an argument with someone and left early. When two others drove Carole home, he met them on the front porch wearing only his underwear in what was described as a "kind of rage."

Another event related in the book had Otto in the attic and somehow cutting his hand, badly, said Knoth, who was over at the house with Otto's son, Neil. When they ran up to the attic, Otto screamed at them to get out and never explained how it happened.

By mid-1971, Carole Nilson had had enough and the couple separated, with Otto moving out. But the violence didn't stop there.

Curt Knoth recalled an incident in which Otto's son, Neil Nilson, went to confront his father in his apartment on Maplewood Avenue in Maplewood, adjacent to his long-time accounting office. He said Otto Nilson eventually attacked his son and got him in a chokehold.

Years later, in 1974, Nilson was arrested after breaking into a neighbor's home in a rage and attacking several people. He was ordered to undergo a psychiatric evaluation after the assaults and ended up with a two-year suspended sentence.

Meanwhile, the artist's sketch of Joan Kramer's killer continued to circulate and spark interest for those who knew Nilson or noticed a resemblance to the South Orange resident and Maplewood accountant.

By January 1975, the woman who had offered the description of the man who picked up Joan Kramer that night in 1972 identified him as Otto Nilson.

Mary Colato of South Orange was the one who described the person she saw giving Kramer a ride, which led to the artist's sketch in the first place. She told police Nilson was the man and they picked him up at his Maplewood apartment/office on Jan. 12, 1975, according to news reports at the time.

He, of course, lived and worked just blocks from where Carol Ann Farino was last seen more than eight years earlier.

A *New York Times* story on the arrest added that Rev. Daniel A. Danik, assistant pastor of Our Lady of Sorrows Church in South Orange, said the Nilsons "had been parishioners of the church for some time" and that "Nilson and his wife had been experiencing domestic difficulties for probably three years."

It also revealed the couple had sought assistance and counseling from the clergy and professional marriage counselors, noting the priest described Nilson as "usually pleasant" and "a fine gentleman."

Several reports also said Nilson had taught religious education classes at the church and served as an usher in the same church that had held Carol's funeral service.

The trial of Otto Neil Nilson began the first week of July 1975 and ran a rollercoaster of accusations, witness testimony, and, in some cases, unclear evidence.

The trial received wide-ranging coverage from many New Jersey outlets, New York tabloids who live for such tawdry and sex-related crime stories, and the Associated Press.

Essex County Superior Court Judge Sam A. Colarusso did not run a strict courtroom, however, allowing some evidence, such as polygraph test results, to be entered into judgment. Such findings are inadmissible today.

He also saw some courtroom directives ignored.

For instance, by the time Nilson came to court he had grown a full beard, changing his visual description from the one he had had back in 1972, and even on the day of his arrest.

When the judge directed him to shave it off, Nilson ignored the order.

During the two-week trial, prosecutors cited two key witnesses—Colato and a man, James Tillett, who worked as a security guard at an apartment building close to where Kramer had been picked up, according to news accounts.

Colato testified that she had seen Nilson driving the car that picked up a woman in an evening gown that night along South Orange Avenue where Kramer was last seen, but could not identify her as Kramer.

Tillett revealed that he was not sure if the man he saw pick up Kramer was Nilson, initially testifying that he had a mustache, but later changing his story and admitting he lied. A police investigator also revealed that Tillett was unable to pick Nilson out of a line-up of photos of 12 men.

Tillett's testimony was later ruled as inadmissible.

Surprisingly, one piece of evidence that was admitted was a police investigator revealing that Colato had failed a polygraph test.

Another strange piece of the trial cited in *Devil's Teeth* involves the alleged actions of South Orange Police Officer Stanley B. Dalton. Colato claimed that she had seen an officer enter a nearby restaurant at the time Nilson allegedly picked up a woman along South Orange Avenue.

Dalton was believed to have been that officer and was called to testify, but on the stand he said he'd never been there that night, citing medical records that he had checked himself into the hospital for an eight-day stay related to addiction.

A Kramer family member told Pollack and Moran that he did not believe Dalton and accused him of sneaking out of the rehab and failing to admit it.

"To this date, many who were close to or involved in the Kramer case felt that Dalton was faced with a difficult choice," according to *Devil's Teeth*. "Rumors about Dalton's alleged alcoholism were flaunted around South Orange, and some feel that this led to his admission into Orange Memorial Hospital for treatment. Some allege that he was able to sneak out of the hospital undetected for a drink at the Bun 'N Burger only one day after becoming a patient, and this was when he witnessed Kramer entering Nilson's car."

There is one problem with that theory: The Bun 'N Burger did not serve alcohol. No further evidence ever tied Dalton to the incident.

It later came out at trial that Nilson had owned a 1964 green Buick at the time of the killing, the same color as the car Colato claimed had picked up Kramer.

At one point, jurors requested a side-by-side comparison of Nilson's photo and the sketch, according to news reports.

After the 14 days of testimony, Judge Colarusso advised the jury that they must choose a verdict of either second-degree murder, manslaughter, or acquittal. He said no first-degree verdict was possible because he did not believe the killing was premeditated.

The jury convened for half of the day on July 15, 1975, before being sent home after a reported argument in the jury room. At least two jurors departed in tears, according to news accounts. The group reconvened the next day and reached a verdict at about 2:30 p.m.: not guilty.

News reports at the time seemed to indicate that there was not enough evidence to convince the jury. The two key witnesses, Colato and Tillett, offered only partial positive identifications, and no other evidence or witness testimony was involved.

Essex County Prosecutor Joseph P. Lordi told the Devil's Teeth authors that he remained convinced that Nilson was Kramer's killer, while Colato reportedly moved across the country to California because she feared retaliation from the suspect.

Her fears that he was dangerous were proven correct just over a year later when Nilson was arrested for holding two doctors hostage and barricading himself inside an East Orange veterans hospital, according to a Sept. 1976 *Passaic Herald-News* story.

Nilson had brought a sniper-scoped rifle with him and took over the facility at 5 a.m. on a Monday after a guard tried to take the weapon away. He eventually took two doctors who had tried to talk him out of the hospital as hostages.

In 1977, Nilson was found not guilty by reason of insanity and committed to the Trenton State Hospital, the same institution that houses Richard Cottingham. He died there on March 2, 1992.

Nilson was never charged in connection with Jeanette De Palma's death despite the close timing, location, and similarities between the De Palma and Joan Kramer killings.

With even fewer clues tying Nilson to De Palma's death, it's not surprising that there was not enough to go on, other than the coincidental timing and close locations. From the beginning, De Palma's murder was an unusual case given that she was found up in the hidden hilltop spot.

It's unlikely she was killed there and, more probably, was carried there by a killer who had to go out of his or her way to reach the spot. Unlike Joan Kramer or Carol Ann Farino, whose bodies were essentially dumped in out-of-the-way places that were easily found, Jeannette De Palma's remains were brought up a hillside and carefully laid out with strange items surrounding them.

In the nearly 50 years since De Palma's death, speculation grew that it might be satanic worshippers. When the stories first hit the newspapers in 1972 and 1973, demonic elements were in the headlines.

"Church of Satan in Jersey gives devil his due," and "Witchcraft implicated in DePalma murder" were among the early headlines after it was revealed that investigators and DePalma's own parents thought there was some kind of satanic link.

In 2019, two major New Jersey papers—*The Star-Ledger* of Newark and the *Central Jersey Home News Tribune*—did special updates on the murder as a cold case, both citing the bizarre theories of her death.

"The country was hurtling towards a satanic panic and the discovery of Jeanette DePalma's body—three months after her disappearance—

could not have been more sinister," *The Star-Ledger* proclaimed. "Police said at the time that someone had placed crosses by the girl's head and used branches to make a coffin-like outline around her body."

The Home News Tribune added, "with a lack of any concrete answers, theories have abounded for decades, ranging from a satanic ritual sacrifice to a coven of witches practicing black magic."

Both papers had renewed interest in the murder because of a lawsuit filed at the time by Ed Salzano, who happened to have grown up in Maplewood and had gotten to know DePalma's nephew, John Bancey, when he moved to Springfield.

Salzano, who was 10 at the time of the murder, said he remembers his parents keeping him home on Halloween the year DePalma died out of fear for him.

His lawsuit sought to force the Springfield Police to conduct DNA testing on DePalma's clothes, something they had not done. (Maplewood police have also failed to do any DNA testing on Carol Ann Farino's clothes or items she wore.)

The lawsuit was dismissed in September 2019.

DePalma's strong religious beliefs were also considered a reason she might have been targeted by satanic worshippers. A website devoted to the victim was launched by Bancey and Salzano several years ago.

JusticeforJeanette.com describes her as "a very religious evangelist who helped lost teenagers find God." It added that she had planned to attend bible college after high school.

The website links to a petition urging that the status of the case be changed from a "suspicious death" to a "homicide." So far, no new evidence or re-opening of the case has occurred.

Nilson also never faced legal charges or increased scrutiny pertaining to Carol Ann Farino's death, even though her killing is nearly always brought up in relation to the DePalma and Kramer murders.

Nilson's connection to Maplewood Village also makes him a prime suspect, given that he had an office across from Milt's Cup & Saucer and down the street from George's Luncheonette when Carol was strangled.

Maplewood Police Detective Christopher Dolias said the file on Carol's murder includes indications that Nilson was under scrutiny once the 1972 killings occurred and later when he was arrested. But he said there was never enough evidence to link him to the crime.

"Otto became the suspect, he was the prime suspect with those (previous) officers," he said. "We didn't have any witnesses. It would be going off of a confession and we never got that."

But did Maplewood Police ever do a door-to-door canvassing of Maplewood Village businesses and apartments after Carol's death? Dolias would not say and since the department refuses to share more information on the decades-old case, it is still unknown.

There is no indication in the few reports that are public or news accounts from the time that any outreach beyond Carol's friends and family was ever done in her case, and if it was it was likely too late to find a stranger who may have left town soon after the murder.

Had police reached out to everyone who either lived in Maplewood Village or worked there, they would have found Otto Neil Nilson who had an office, and later an apartment, above 173 Maplewood Ave.

Cynthia Farino believes such scrutiny would have tied Nilson to Milt's Cup & Saucer where Carol worked because she had told the family about a man who fit his description and would visit the eatery regularly.

"She had told my mother about this nice man who used to come in and talk to her every day, he was very religious," Cynthia said about the man believed to be Nilson, at the time a religious education teacher at Our Lady of Sorrows Church. "She said he was very nice and none of us thought anything about it until later."

Nilson had a reputation for working with many of the OLS students, as some of Carol's friends remembered. Several told me that he would volunteer at nearby South Orange dances and other events as a chaperone or volunteer.

Even if Carol's friends and family believed adamantly that she would not have willingly gotten into a car with a stranger on the night she died, Cynthia believed she might have taken a ride on a cold night from Nilson or other Milt's customers if they were regulars and she felt they could be trusted.

In another possible scenario, a Milt's customer who was attracted to Carol might have followed her home. After seeing the route she normally took up Maplewood Avenue, the person could have chosen a later night to wait for her on the side of the road with a plan to grab her or pretend to have seen her by chance.

"He probably came by and offered her a ride, or if he was waiting and stalking her, that might have been him," Cynthia theorized about Nilson. "They should have looked into it when he was arrested, but they didn't. They might have thought he was a good candidate, but the police let it slide. I don't think they looked too hard."

Once Nilson was arrested in 1975, Cynthia said the Maplewood Police should have done everything to link him to Carol's death. But she believes they were still stuck on her father as a suspect despite his alibis.

"Absolutely, when [Nilson] got arrested I decided for sure that I didn't think my father did it, because of the timing issues," Cynthia said. "They rehashed the whole thing all over again and I was old enough to pick up the whole thing on my own. They were so dead set on my dad."

Chapter Twelve

Mark Allegri came into Cynthia's life at a time when her relationships were changing fast. She had separated from Nick, and Daniel remained on-again, off-again.

Ann and Frank Farino had moved back to New Jersey years earlier, settling in the Jersey Shore town of Whiting, part of Manchester Township in Ocean County, a far cry from Maplewood's small town and paranoid police probes. Both had had enough of their past in Essex County and felt more comfortable in new surroundings, where a false suspicion of murder did not hang over Frank's head.

For Cynthia, that meant a mixed bag of less parental oversight and influence, but no direct family members nearby. So when Mark approached her one night in a Kansas City bar in 1988, she was ripe for some new romantic support.

"We went through five or six bottles of champagne, the waiters were having the best time waiting on us," she recalls about how the evening began with a visiting Angela and another friend. "We decided to leave and go to another bar."

Soon after arriving at the second spot, Mark swooped in.

"We just saw him and he started to talk to us with his friend, I think Angela liked him more than I did," she remembers. "I wasn't sure about him. Then we hung out at the hotel that night. He was the type who wouldn't leave you alone. I just couldn't get rid of him, but he was very nice."

That nice guy image would change to clinging and overbearing. Cynthia soon grew tired of it, but in her vulnerable and mixed-up state, she could not let go.

Cynthia Farino, late 1980s

In 1990, she and Nick finally divorced, but she remained in Missouri with good work and an active social life. Her nights included Mark and other gentlemen callers, but nothing that seemed serious.

Then Mark got pushy, almost possessive, and wanted to move in with her. "That was a mistake of my life. I didn't want to date anymore so I figured I would give him a chance," Cynthia said. "Big mistake."

Cynthia and Mark had started a produce delivery business together, so moving in seemed the thing to do, despite his signs of being outlandishly demanding and always on a power trip.

"It was a while that we were together, maybe two years," she said. "I just couldn't get rid of him. My father totally hated him."

The produce business was doing okay, but nothing great, and Mark gave it as little effort as possible. He seemed to spend more time trying to control Cynthia and track her movements.

At one point, she escaped to Club Med in Cancun with Angela for a 10-day holiday. "Part of it was just to get away from him," she said. "I had to get away."

One of the rules of Club Med was no phones and limited outside interference, as much for the guests to be able to detach from their busy lives as for the staff to concentrate on making them feel at home.

But that was not enough for Mark to stay away. Cynthia recalls he would call constantly and even break into the hotel switchboards with emergency calls. "He would not leave me alone, I think they were glad to get rid of me when we left because he was always calling," she said.

But it only got worse when they landed back in Kansas City. Mark was waiting with his mother, a limousine, and a marriage proposal. He also carried a video camera and taped the entire proceeding. He had warned Angela that he was going to do it and she tried to stop him.

"I was pretty disgusted because I just wanted out. I said 'yes' just because I didn't want to embarrass him in front of his mother," Cynthia said. "It was over the top and it was tacky, very tacky."

Once they returned home, Mark pushed for a wedding date, but Cynthia stalled. She used her recent divorce as an excuse for not rushing back into marriage, while secretly trying to figure out how to get out of it all.

"I was not going to plan anything, I was not going to marry him, but I had to figure out how," she said. "It was not the greatest situation and he started going out and staying out all night sometimes. At one point I just threw his stuff out, but I let him back in because I was in business with him and had money invested."

Cynthia soon found out that some of Mark's friends were local hoods mixed up in illegal activities, but she was not sure what—possibly drugs or stolen items. She suspected drugs when he went out and stayed away overnight with no explanation. He also did not focus on work or their relationship.

"He was still living with me, but it was not working out," Cynthia recalls. "He was very charming in the beginning, but when he moved in I started to wonder what he was doing."

The tragic and bizarre ending came on the night of Oct. 4, 1991, when Mark went out and did not come back even the next day. Cynthia was so sick of his antics and lack of honesty that she did not even give it much of a thought when he never returned. She assumed he had been seeing another woman or engaged in some kind of illegal activity.

"I woke up in the middle of the night and Mark was still out, I could not find him so I went to sleep," she recalled. "I got up the next day and went to work where I was still doing facials."

She assumed she would find him later and let him have it for yet another irresponsible act.

But when Mark's brother, Michael, appeared at the store she knew it was something else. He told her that Mark had been shot and killed.

News accounts from the incident said Mark had likely been seeking to buy illegal drugs in the city's high crime Marlboro Heights area where the killing occurred. He was found at about 10:30 p.m. slumped over the steering wheel of a white car with a bullet wound to the head. Police had initially responded to an auto accident after he crashed the van into a pole.

Soon after his death, police arrested two teens who lived in a nearby apartment building and had spotted Mark from their window.

One of the teens told police they meant to frighten him with a gunshot and then rob him, but they accidentally killed him. A *Kansas City Star* story noted that the suspects said they had been told by a friend that Mark was known to carry drug-buying money and wear a lot of jewelry, both of which would be ripe for stealing.

The suspects, Kevin Pewitte, 19, and Elroy Washington, 15, were later charged with first-degree murder and second-degree murder, respectively, and both faced an added charge of armed criminal action.

Washington was eventually charged as an adult despite being a minor after a judge noted his past involvement in auto tampering and armed robbery, saying he had a "general disposition to resolve social or personal problems in ways that show disregard for social customs or rules" and that "he is especially prone toward involvement in drug-related crimes."

Cynthia said it was a shock, but not completely surprising given Mark's continued secrecy and lack of responsibility. She said she had wanted the relationship to end and felt relieved.

"I wanted out so badly to get away from him. I could have thrown a party when he was shot, that's how relieved I was," she recalls. "I was sad for him and I was shocked more than anything. I felt sorry for his family because they were a wreck."

Cynthia called Angela to let her know what happened. The two had spent the previous months commiserating over the relationship: "When I told her he had died, she said, 'you must have had an angel on your shoulder.'"

In 1992, Cynthia was back in the Garden State for another CHS reunion, this time the 20th anniversary. There was Daniel once again at a pre-reunion gathering the night before.

"We had seen each other and talked on the phone occasionally and once he saw me he came right to me," she said about the re-connection. "We left together and he showed me the house he had bought in Jersey City."

That's all it took and the couple found love and lust again, at least for that night and the days that followed. Cynthia went to the reunion and they spent most of the time together, as well as a few days after.

"I wasn't going to move back just for him and change my life for him," she said.

So she stayed in Kansas City and wound up in yet another unhealthy relationship with a charming, trouble-bound man. "Kevin," a car salesman, worked his way into Cynthia's life and even convinced her to move with him to Arizona in the spring of 1992.

"I think I was very adventurous, I never gave it a lot of thought, I never thought through things," she said. "Maybe I was unsettled. I thought I didn't want to be there anymore, in Kansas City."

So the couple relocated to Scottsdale, an affluent desert hub known for its meditation history and relaxing options.

"I thought I could move anywhere I wanted," she said. "It was very hard to get a job there, I was not happy with him anyway so I started making plans behind his back to leave. I was also talking to Daniel on and off by phone."

Kevin's compulsive gambling also became a problem: "He would bet on anything, and his friends were sick, too. He lost a lot of money."

After about five months it got to be too much, so she just jumped in her car one day, dropped him off at work, and drove back to Kansas City without telling Kevin: "Daniel thought I was going to drive straight through to New Jersey, which I should have, but I didn't."

During that stretch of her life—from high school through her first marriage, a whirlwind affair, moving back and forth from the Midwest and landing alone as a divorced single woman in the middle of the country—Cynthia's thoughts always went to Carol.

"I always thought about her and wondered about her," she said. "All the time I would think about her. And I would wonder what happened?"

She believed her jumping from relationship to relationship and often with poor choices was a result, in part, of what happened to Carol.

"I wouldn't have done any of this stuff," she believes. "I would have been a different person. I would not have wanted to move out of Maplewood in the first place, I would have been another person."

"I always thought about her around the holidays, how different my life would have been, and if she had been here," Cynthia said. "Maybe I would have been different. She was more able to conform than me and it made me struggle without her."

"I would have been a totally different person if this did not happen. I changed drastically because of this."

Hoping for some kind of guidance and contact with her departed sibling, Cynthia visited a medium for the first time in Kansas City after a friend recommended it in the late 1980s.

"She used to go to one and she thought it might help me out," Cynthia recalls. "But she never said anything about my sister, it was more about me and what was going on in my life."

"She was good, but it was mostly about things that were going to happen in my life and did happen. She talked a lot about my health and wanted me to quit smoking. She told me things to be aware of, she told me I would eventually marry someone who was very kind, who wore glasses, and did not live in Kansas City."

Once she returned from Arizona, Cynthia gave Kansas City one more go of it, continuing to work at a day spa inside a Saks Fifth Avenue in the Plaza area of Kansas City.

She still liked that neighborhood, especially at holiday time when the Christmas lights spruced up the retail sections and music played. "It was so beautiful with the lights, it was amazing."

After a while, she sold the house and moved to a smaller apartment in Overland Park, Kansas, outside of the city.

"The area we had lived in, Grandview, Missouri, was starting to change and become unsafe," Cynthia remembers. "Overland Park was fun and there were a lot of places to shop. It was the place to be."

Nick stayed in the area and remarried, she heard, but they never reconnected. Still, working and meeting new people kept Cynthia busy and in touch, with a friendly roommate, regular visits from Angela and some New Jersey friends, as well as socializing with new acquaintances, and dates.

Eventually, she met Angelo, who was the cousin of a co-worker at a dating service that briefly employed Cynthia as the manager of cold-calling prospective clients. She was not crazy about the job, given the hours and demand for new clients.

"We had to work on Sundays and I hated it because you couldn't go out on Saturday night and have fun," she remembers. "Angelo was my roommate's cousin, that's how I met him. His mother ran a cleaning business that he worked with and I used to help her once in a while and that is how I got into the cleaning business."

After a while, the cleaning operation took off, and Cynthia was able to pay the rent and bills on her cleaning income, while her relationship with Angelo grew. She even moved in with him for a year, but it turned out to be another wrong turn.

"I wasn't in love with him, I realized I wasn't going anywhere with him, he was also 12 years older than me," she recalled. "I was just not happy then, I decided it was time to go, but I did not want to go home then. I avoided it to stay away from my parents, I did not want to live with them."

Cynthia was stuck, both emotionally and physically, feeling she could not return to New Jersey and be under her parents' control and verbal harangues. But she hated the idea of staying with Angelo and in a place that had never seemed to work out.

And what if Carol were here? What would she tell her to do? Or advise her to try? Or maybe just give her a big-sister hug and hope. That empty place in her life only grew more painful when tough decisions and circumstances arose.

At one point, Angelo finally gave her the push she needed to get out when he showed his true irresponsibility.

"He was a terrible nasty drunk. One night we were out together and as we walked out of a bar he was talking to somebody and got mad at them," Cynthia remembers. "He broke a beer bottle on a car, the glass flew up and cut my face. I had to drive myself to the emergency room. He was drunk and I had to drop him off at home first."

Soon after, in another argument between the couple, Angelo struck Cynthia and she slapped him back.

That was it.

"I threw my clothes in the car and drove back to New Jersey," she said. Grabbing what she could, Cynthia piled her belongings into her white Ford Probe and hit the road for the 1,200-mile journey.

Cynthia's years in Kansas City were a mix of bad relationships and an atmosphere of mistrust and a midwestern prejudice she never saw in New Jersey, she said.

"It was so prejudicial if you are different, and there was a lot of antisemitism," she recalled. "I couldn't believe it was like that. Living in Kansas City was no fun, I was an oddity there. If you weren't blonde you were strange. Everyone was toilet-seat white blonde. After a while it was boring, I stayed there because I didn't want to come home to my parents."

But with few choices about her next options for money and a home, and her aging parents longing for their only daughter to help care for them, Cynthia set out in her car on a chilly October afternoon in 1994.

"I did 12-hour days," she recalls. "I just wanted to get out of there. I was done with Kansas City, I was never going to go back, I was coming home. I was just done with it. I wasn't sad about leaving, that's for sure."

The last thing she wanted to do was live with her parents. Memories of their abusive language and neglectful approach, as well as Carol's still unsolved death, gnawed at her the entire way and created a reality she was not looking forward to.

She didn't even tell Angelo her plans and made the decision to move on a bit of a spur of the moment, although the itch to depart had been there for a while.

"He didn't know, when I'm done with somebody, I'm done," she said. "If I don't care about you, there's no explanations offered. I just wanted to go home, I was done. When I left Arizona I should have just gone home, I realized, but I ended up staying in Kansas City for another year and a half."

As Cynthia steered her car east on I-70 that calm fall day, her mind raced from thoughts of the broken relationships she left behind to the potential stress of family that lay ahead. And, of course, returning to the state where some of her worst memories were contained, the most notable the continued mystery over Carol's death.

"I always thought about her, what she would have thought. She would have been happy for me I think," she mused.

Cynthia wanted so badly to get through the trip quickly that she sped across the countryside almost without stopping, spending just one night in a nondescript Ohio motel and logging two long days.

Once she reached Pennsylvania, Cynthia's mood brightened. "It was beautiful in the fall, Pennsylvania was beautiful. Prettier than in Kansas City, where everything always looked dirty, and then muddy when it rained.

"I remember I had to call my father to tell me where to get off the Pennsylvania Turnpike," she said about her final hours approaching New Jersey. "He had to give me directions. He was glad I was coming home. They were both glad. But because they needed me, they needed help."

When she finally entered New Jersey, one quick incident confirmed she was home: "When I hit the Jersey Turnpike, I said 'Hi' to the toll taker and he said, 'Yeah, right lady,'" Cynthia remembers. "I started laughing because it meant I was back. I was really happy about it."

Even before her break from Angelo and quick decision to leave Missouri, Cynthia had been getting the message from her mother about a need to come back.

"My father was sick already, congestive heart failure, and my mother kept hinting that he couldn't do anything anymore," she said. "And since my mother still never learned to drive, they were stuck. They were happy to have me now because they had someone to take care of things they couldn't do anymore."

Not exactly a glowing homecoming, Cynthia thought, but somewhat cordial anyway. When Cynthia finally arrived, she found her Aunt Rose and Uncle Ernie visiting for dinner and they all gave her a warm reception.

"It was a big thing. I came in late, it was after dark, about 8 o'clock or 9 o'clock," she said. "It was after dinner and they were playing cards."

But after a few days, the new reality began. Frank Farino was facing health issues that all but kept him housebound, while Ann was limited in being able to help him because of her age and lack of a driver's license.

Cynthia had become their go-to aide.

"My father was still his nasty, nasty self, but I didn't take any shit from him," she said. "I would tell him to be quiet."

Unable to get a New Jersey cosmetology license or afford the classes needed to obtain one, Cynthia had to give up her esthetician career and take the other work route she knew: home cleaning.

She eventually launched a cleaning business to help with the bills and it did well. "I wasn't happy about it, I needed money, and I knew I needed to start soon. I wanted to get out of my parents' house as soon as possible."

Outside socializing was put on hold.

"I didn't get in touch with anybody for about a year, not even Daniel," she said. "I had bouts of depression where I just couldn't deal with anyone and did not want to deal with anything."

Cynthia's milestone birthday was on November 12, 1994. But she saw no reason to mark the occasion. "I didn't do anything, I didn't even celebrate it, I was not happy. I was burned out, I just wanted to be left alone."

Cynthia did have some fun moments, such as the time she and Ann went to the ASPCA in Toms River to get a cat for Frank that Christmas. They named her Jenny. "They didn't tell us she was going to have kittens, so when she had them they were so cute and we almost were going to keep all of them."

They gave away three of them and ended up with Jenny and one kitten, dubbed Fluffy. "They were all of our cats, they slept with me at night, they loved me."

At one point in the mid-1990s, about 30 years after Carol's murder, the family heard from Maplewood Police. But when Ann answered the phone, the detective on the other end offered no word on any clues, suspects, or progress, just a message that the cops had not forgotten about the case.

"She hung up on them," Cynthia recalls. "She was so disgusted with them. How dare they even call here."

After about a year of being home, Cynthia called Daniel and they reconnected. But an affair that had begun some 12 years earlier would soon die out. "He started telling me to stay with him on the weekends, which I did."

Then a bombshell dropped when Cynthia discovered he had been seeing another woman at the same time. The revelation occurred while Daniel was out of his house and Cynthia was taking a shower.

When she stepped out, there was a woman in his bedroom asking for Daniel. "That's when it was over," she recalled. "And I left and never saw him again."

When Cynthia got home, Daniel called her and said he was not happy about the woman's visit and it would never happen again. But Cynthia wasn't buying it. "Something just snapped and I thought, 'Fuck you!' You have been trying to tell me who you are for 12 years and I decided it was just over."

Cynthia would think about him over the years but never reached out. News would come through the grapevine that he had gotten married, with kids, in Maplewood and ran his own cleaning business that still operates today.

"I always loved him, I could never stop no matter who else came along," she revealed. "I never really got over it, but I forced myself not to get in touch with him. I knew I had to get over this, it had to be over."

But for the next 20 years, Daniel stayed in her thoughts, prompting Cynthia to occasionally track down how he was doing and what happened to him, but she held back trying to reach him.

Shockingly, she did not discover his death until 2020, a few months after it happened when she did an online search and stumbled upon his obituary.

"I was devastated. It was over for sure, I would never see him again," she said. "You don't really change when you get older. I didn't really ever think about him being married to someone else, that really gets to me."

Chapter Thirteen

John Perna was born a year before Carol Ann Farino's killing.

And although he grew up in Maplewood, walked the same streets as her, and also attended Columbia High School, he never learned about her murder case until he became a township police officer himself in 1988.

"It's not something that was really talked about a whole lot. We knew it was a homicide, but no details or anything like that," he said about what he learned of the murder case during his first days on the job. "We knew there was a homicide in Maplewood Center, we knew the location of it. Just some basic information about it and where they found the body."

"But that's about it. There is not much more than that. We did not know what steps were taken, what agencies were used, what Maplewood's role was, or what the prosecutor's office was doing."

One of three brothers who grew up in Maplewood and attended CHS, Perna was a standout offensive and defensive lineman on the football team and a popular student. He was named an all-state player, team MVP, and led the Cougars to the Iron Hills Championship game as a senior.

His skill and experience earned Perna an athletic scholarship to the University of Maryland, where his gridiron teammates included future Super Bowl quarterback Boomer Esiason and NFL head coach Frank Reich.

When the NFL did not come calling, Perna pursued an interest in law enforcement after earning a bachelor's degree in political science. He entered the Union County Police Academy in nearby Scotch Plains, N.J., graduating after 24 weeks.

The academy, later named after respected Union County Prosecutor John Stamler, is among the highest-rated law enforcement institutions of learning in the nation. One of Stamler's last public appearances before his death from a heart ailment was Perna's 1988 graduation.

Perna joined the Maplewood police force soon after his academy work was completed and spent the next 25 years among the township's men in blue, eventually rising to the rank of detective bureau commander. In that post, he would have direct oversight of all unsolved cases, Farino's killing among them.

But when Perna first put on the uniform in the late 1980s there was another unsolved murder case in town that drew attention for its organized crime ties, blatant ruthlessness, and murder-for-hire origins.

The "Pizza Killing," as it was dubbed, even sounded like a mob movie or an episode of *The Sopranos*, with everything except a theme song.

Edward Potcher, 37, owned Jack's Pizzeria at the corner of Springfield and Boyden avenues in Maplewood when he was shot four times at close range on August 12, 1986, in the pizzeria. He died just hours later.

But the gunman and the motive were a mystery for more than a year since there was no evidence tying anyone to the crime and no money went missing from the cash register.

It was also the first murder in town since Carol's death almost 20 years earlier, giving cops two unsolved killings to examine, although it appears Carol's death had been set aside even then.

Given its near-Hollywood drama storyline and involvement of a local popular pizza shop owner, the Potcher killing received both strong media attention and detective priorities.

As Perna studied his books and procedures in the police academy through 1987 and the beginning of 1988, Maplewood Police focused on both associates and customers of Potcher, which spanned much of Essex County and Northern New Jersey.

Eventually, the case found its way to New York City when a 26-year-old small-time criminal named Anthony DiFrisco was arrested for traffic violations and car theft. Scared and nervous about facing prison for a felony, DiFrisco tried to bargain his way out of it by implicating a "higher-up" in the criminal world.

DiFrisco eventually confessed to shooting Potcher in a scheme that paid him just $2,500 from a known mob associate named Anthony Franciotti.

Court papers recounted DiFrisco's conversation with Bronx Detective Harry Kukk at the time when he asked if a hitman would be more prosecuted than the man who hired him.

> *And he asked me, he said, "Harry, who is more guilty, a guy who shoots a guy or a guy who pays him to shoot the guy?"*
>
> *I said, "I have no problem. A guy who pays him to shoot the guy."*
>
> *He said, "Are you serious?"*
>
> *I said, "Sure."*
>
> *"The guy who killed the guy is only an intermediate, only a pawn."*
>
> *He said, "Harry, I don't know whether to trust you or not. If I tell you something, you are not going to ram it down me."*

That led to DiFrisco's confession and eventual arrest.

Franciotti had been known in New York crime and law enforcement circles for years, with at least one past conviction for robbery. He was also allegedly the "mastermind" behind a 1972 attempted kidnapping of a Manhattan contracting company executive that involved four other associates, all later arrested as well.

Court papers revealed that Franciotti had met DiFrisco in jail years earlier and later approached him to kill Potcher, after fearing the pizza shop owner would reveal Franciotti's illegal activities to the police.

It is unclear how Potcher had come to find out about Franciotti's crimes and background or how well they knew each other.

DiFrisco, an admitted drug abuser and petty criminal, initially recalled few details about the "pizza killing" to cops, failing to remember even where it took place. New York detectives began scouring records and touching base with New Jersey authorities after the killer admitted it had been a Garden State homicide.

"Bit by bit, the New York police closed in on the case. They called New Jersey authorities. They found an unsolved murder in Maplewood fitting the description of the murder in respect of time and place," one court record of the case stated. Maplewood Police found that the case resembled the Potcher shooting too much to be a coincidence.

DiFrisco's recollections noted that the deadly shots were fired from a .32 caliber automatic with a silencer. The final clue might have come when the killer recalled that the pizzeria did not sell slices, only whole pizza pies.

Maplewood Police and investigators from the Essex County Prosecutor's office eventually arrived at the Bronx precinct where DiFrisco repeated the story to them and later signed a confession to the murder implicating Franciotti.

One report even claimed cops tied DiFrisco to the killing by matching his teeth to bite marks on a slice he purchased the day of the murder.

He said Franciotti had paid him to commit the murder because "the pizza shop owner was about to inform on Franciotti," according to court records. DiFrisco described how Franciotti drove him to Maplewood on the day of the murder and stayed in the car as DiFrisco walked into the pizzeria alone and fired the fatal shots. Afterward, he said, Franciotti drove them both back to Manhattan.

Investigators said they needed to get proof that Franciotti had ordered the hit and arranged for DiFrisco to call him and have the conversation taped while Franciotti hopefully admitted guilt during the call.

DiFrisco had been given a public defender who advised him to make the call. But at the last moment he refused, saying his father had counseled against further cooperation with the police without a paid personal lawyer involved.

Investigators determined they could not arrest Franciotti on the word of DiFrisco alone and, lacking any other direct evidence, he was never charged. But a grand jury eventually indicted DiFrisco on a lone charge of first-degree murder that sought the death penalty

Court records stated, "the aggravating factors noted were that '[t]he murder was outrageously or wantonly vile'; that the defendant was paid to commit the murder, and that the murder was committed to escape the detection of another crime."

Faced with evidence that included his confession, DiFrisco went to court on Jan. 11, 1988, and pled guilty to murder. He repeated his confession after being asked specifically, "Was it your intention to kill him at that time?" His answer: "Yes."

DiFrisco then waived his right to a jury trial for the penalty phase, in which it is decided if he should receive the death penalty. State law requires that such a question be offered to a jury unless the defendant chooses otherwise.

DiFrisco believed that he might have a better chance with the judge given his claims that police coerced him into believing he would receive a lighter punishment if he implicated Franciotti.

Prosecutors cited the three factors of pre-planning, murder for hire, and cover-up noted above in their case, as well as the confession and forensic evidence found at the scene, according to court documents.

But DiFrisco's lawyers cited the fact that the case was still "under investigation" and said it would not be proper to sentence him to death if the case is not considered closed.

In the end, however, the judge sentenced DiFrisco to death and he was placed on New Jersey's death row in 1988. His request for a new trial was denied and an appeal was later rejected by the New Jersey State Supreme Court in 1990.

However, in a dissenting opinion, one of the state Supreme Court justices criticized local investigators and prosecutors for failing to seek charges against Franciotti, claiming there was enough evidence to prompt further inquiries and a possible indictment.

"The prosecutor maintained that DiFrisco refused to cooperate and 'stonewalled' the investigation of Franciotti and, further, that DiFrisco's Franciotti story is unbelievable," the dissent said in part. "The trial court eviscerated the prosecutor's explanation: it found that defendant rendered substantial assistance to the State in the prosecution of another person for the crime of murder sufficient to constitute a mitigating factor... For the reasons stated herein, and my belief that the capital-murder statute is invalid, I would vacate defendant's guilty plea, reverse defendant's conviction for murder, and reverse the death sentence."

But DiFrisco remained on death row for the next 16 years until the death sentence was overturned in 2006 by the state Supreme Court. He was resentenced to life in prison in 2007 and stayed locked up until his parole in 2019.

It is unclear how a man who committed a cold-blooded murder and sat on death row for more than a dozen years was found safe to be released.

During the next three decades following the Potcher killing, Maplewood experienced 20 murders—ranging from a triple-homicide drug deal gone wrong to a love triangle involving a jealous boyfriend who stabbed to death his au pair ex-lover and her employer.

Perna responded to some of those cases as an officer and, as he rose through the ranks to detective, he oversaw others. As of 2021, all of the killings had been solved and most involved killers and victims who knew each other.

Except for the 2000 murder of Christine Burns, which I wrote about at the time and mentioned earlier. Her killing was unsolved for nearly three years until DNA evidence that the Essex County Prosecutors Office had ignored for years was finally checked against the state DNA database. It led to her killer being found and convicted in 2003.

Only Carol Ann Farino's death remains a mystery among Maplewood killings.

Perna said it's up to the Essex County Prosecutor's Office whether such a case can be re-opened and reviewed. Technically, it is still an active case, according to Perna and the Prosecutor's Office.

"The Essex County Prosecutor's Office has jurisdiction over all homicides. Even if we did have information, it would have to be presented to the prosecutor's office to see if they would re-open the case," Perna said.

County officials used that claim when they denied both Cynthia Farino and me access to the investigatory files. (More on that later).

Perna said that even as an officer, he would not have been given much information on a murder case, especially one as old as the Farino killing.

"You don't really have access to that information if you are outside of the detective bureau. Because in our investigative division everything is confidential, you are not really privy to that information unless you are a supervisor in the detective bureau," he explained. "There would have been times when there were different leaders who wanted to re-examine evidence, that is the kind of stuff that may have occurred. But Maplewood has no authority to reopen anything."

Perna, now a North Carolina attorney specializing in trust, estate, and corporate law, said that there was a small wave of young girl murders in Northern New Jersey in the late 1960s and early 1970s, several mentioned in earlier chapters. He said Maplewood likely followed leads on each one that could have resembled the Farino killing.

"There were a lot of things going on outside of Maplewood when the homicide occurred, there weren't suspects in the Maplewood murder, but there were several small-town incidents in the Northern New Jersey area, so over time I am sure they were all looked at as potential suspects," he said. "Any female that was murdered, that person would have been looked at by investigators at the time."

But none of those efforts proved successful in tying any suspects to Carol's death.

Then, in 2011, Perna got his own chance to take a look at the case. That's when he became Maplewood Police detective bureau commander, the highest post in the bureau. Among the cases he sought to review was Farino's.

"Whenever a detective commander takes over, they give it a review and that is what I did," he told me. "Each time a new commander comes into the detective bureau they will open that case to take a look at it to see what has been done, what could be done. Just generally speaking and I can't say that every commander has done this, when you come into the detective bureau it is your responsibility to take a look at that. It is a kind of changing of the guards. I can't speak to what previous commanders or the ones that have come after me have done. But from what I understand, most people would look at that, it is reviewed to see what could be done."

Perna said he went through the case and even made some inquiries, although he offered no details.

"I looked through the files and saw what had been done and saw if anyone had done anything prior to me," he explained. "We talked to some people, the problem was the time delay, the time frame. Many of the people that were living at the time had passed away, so even when we tried to talk to people to get some context, who might have known the family, there was not a whole lot to talk to. Others who knew of the family did not want to talk about it."

Perna declined to offer specific names or examples of those who were approached and also would not comment on any efforts to test DNA from the crime scene or the status of Carol's clothes that were initially kept by cops.

"It is always an open case, there is no statute of limitation on homicides, they never close the case," he said.

But he also noted that more cannot be done without the prosecutor's office and at the time Maplewood Police had no more evidence with which to approach county investigators.

"You have to present something to cause them to consider that new information has been developed, otherwise they weren't going to open the case up," Perna said. "They may have their own cold case unit that may want to review it, but from our department, you have to have something that has changed and see whether or not they want to pursue it or handle it."

A request for an update or comment from the Essex County Prosecutor's Office in late 2020 on Farino's death drew a one-line response from spokeswoman Katherine Carter that said it is essentially always under review. "We are reviewing the case," she said via email. "Homicide cases are never closed unless there is an arrest or some other resolution."

Perna was not surprised at the status of the case and said that as time goes on it gets harder to find new clues.

"Today you probably have a very few people who know about that case, you have had a major turnover of officers, most officers are not from Maplewood," he said. "And during the time that I was coming in, we still had a significant number of older people who were experienced officers who were from Maplewood. But I think people from that time ended with my class, people that would have been born and raised in South Orange and Maplewood."

Perna left the Maplewood Police department in 2013, later moving to North Carolina and joining the law firm.

"A police officer's life is not longevity on the job, it is a rough job," said the married father of three. "I wanted to be able to move into another career, have something lined up."

But the unsolved death of Carol Ann Farino is never far from his thoughts.

"Nobody wants to have a case that you can't solve, it's not something that we want," Perna admitted. "There is a lot of concern and there is no incident where you do not want to see justice served."

Another veteran Maplewood investigator who shares that view is Kevin Kisch. The son of a former Maplewood detective, Kisch grew up in the town just as Perna did. Also one of three sons, Kisch graduated from Columbia High School in 1986, three years after Perna, and later joined the force in 1995.

But unlike Perna, Kisch had essentially grown up under the mystery of Carol Ann Farino, since his father was on the police force in 1966 when her killing occurred.

"If you were a cop who grew up in Maplewood, you knew about the Carol Farino murder," said Kisch, who climbed the ranks to detective and retired as a captain in 2019. "A lot of our parents knew about it and were in Maplewood when it happened."

Although Kevin Kisch wasn't born yet when Carol was strangled, his father, Joseph "Peter" Kisch, was on the police force at the time, having joined in 1964 after graduating from Columbia High School himself. Peter later rose to detective in 1968 and remained on the job until his death in 1989, just six months before retirement.

"In conversations with my mom, she would say, 'Maybe you can solve it in your career,'" Kisch said. "It was always a topic of conversation. Maplewood is a sleepy little town and I think some people thought her father was involved."

Kisch's family lived on tiny Marion Place, about eight blocks from where Carol's body was found. He said he would always think of her if he had to travel past the location or respond to a call nearby.

"Every time I visit or go by that house I look at that corner and think of her," he said. "The story is one that my mom used to tell about that murder and what the scuttlebutt was around town. That you have an innocent girl, a diner waitress walking home, and someone that no one knows just abducts her and drops her blocks away. It was unusual."

The case also remained a topic of conversation in both Kisch households, with his mother and his own recollections.

"I remember my mom talking about it, she would talk about a conversation they would have, her and my father," Kisch said. "I thought about it often only from the emotional side of it, I would love to be able to find the suspect and solve it.

"When I thought of the victim, I thought how unfortunate this was. When you look at someone who is just completely innocent and one night in their life they make a certain turn, they run into a person who is going to end their life and change their path."

Kisch recalled when Perna looked into the case again years ago and remembers that Otto Nilson's name was raised one more time as a possible suspect.

"I remember when he wanted to break open this file, look it over again," Kisch said. "I remember having a conversation with John and about linking it to the guy who [was accused of] kill[ing] the girl in South Orange."

But former South Orange Police Officer Bill Kuhl, Jr. may have the best insight into both Carol Ann Farino and Otto Neil Nilson. A 1967 graduate of Columbia High School, he was a classmate of Carol's for several years and among those affected when she died.

"It was a shock, everybody was sad, it hit like a ton of bricks and back then there were no answers," said Kuhl. "She did nothing to anybody, she would give you the shirt off her back. Carol was the girl every mother wanted her son to bring home. She was always a very studious girl and worked hard."

Years later, Kuhl joined the South Orange Police Department and served from 1971 to 1981. He was on the job when Joan Kramer was murdered and later when Nilson was eventually arrested.

He recalls setting up roadblocks around South Orange shortly after Kramer's death to question residents and seek to catch the killer.

"For what we had I think we did the best we could," he said about the investigation that led to Nilson's capture but failed to convict him. "We did good because they weren't afraid to call in outside help."

But Nilson's arrest was not the first time that Kuhl came across the suspect. He said the man was known at Our Lady of Sorrows Church, where Kuhl attended school for nine years and also served as an altar boy.

"He was weird. He was an oddball, there was something wrong with him and you kept your distance from him," Kuhl recalls about the man who would volunteer at the church and the local Knights of Columbus. "I know Neil wasn't too stable mentally."

But the church's tight-knit community likely blocked efforts to speak out against Nilson, the veteran officer said.

When Nilson's arrest prompted questions about his possible involvement in Carol's murder, Kuhl was not shocked: "No, it was not a surprise because he was strange. If you said he did it, it didn't surprise me, it didn't surprise me that they suspected him because he was that type of a person, that oddness about him."

"Looking back, it very well could have been. You know how a person sends vibes out, you want to stay away from them. That's the way he was. That was my own personal feelings about the man."

Kuhl's feelings about Otto Neil Nilson and his possible ties to Carol's death would not be the last to be raised in the case.

Chapter Fourteen

As 1994 turned into 1995, Cynthia Farino's life took on a new status with fresh horizons, but also some definite uncertainty. She'd been divorced for five years and relocated from a smaller midwestern town where she had independence to an older Jersey Shore community that stuck her with two aging parents and a trunkload of emotional baggage.

Aside from the daily reminders of Carol's mysterious death, Cynthia had her cleaning business to run and her parents' mix of health issues and internal squabbling as they grew older and more cranky.

"I was taking care of her all of those years, it was drudgery," Cynthia said about her mother. "I had a full-time business to run and take care of her. I think she had borderline personality disorder. It was all about her all the time."

Ann and Frank Farino were also still dealing with Carol's death on a near-daily basis with guilt, anger, and some frustration, even when Maplewood Police called to tell them they "had not forgotten about it" but still offered no clues or new information.

"My mother said she didn't want anything to do with it," Cynthia said about the poor police updates. "I was still mad at them for not having an attorney for my parents when they questioned them again and again."

As 1995 wore on, Cynthia grew her cleaning operation at a very productive rate, landing more and more customers and building up a respectable pool of regular clients.

"It really took off right, but I didn't like the caliber of people," she said. "So I started doing people in wealthier towns where I could charge quite a bit more."

Then she met one customer who would change her life forever.

Michael Smith, a local Xerox office machine technician, was some six years younger than Cynthia. His boss at the time happened to hire Cynthia's service to clean his home in Jackson, N.J., known to many as the hometown of Six Flags Great Adventure.

"His manager thought I was a great person and wondered why I wasn't married," she recalls. "He introduced me to another guy and I told him no. Then he gave a different guy my number."

Michael lived in Middletown, about an hour north of Cynthia's parents' home in Whiting. He called her soon after being told about her and suggested getting together. Handsome, friendly, and hard-working, Michael drew her in, but with some hesitation given her checkered past with men.

"I wasn't sure what I wanted to do because I had been in love with Daniel," Cynthia said. "He was very charming and very, very funny and had a great sense of humor. He was such a nice person and I could tell. I told him I was not in a hurry and neither was he because he had gotten divorced."

And even as she had sworn off Daniel to his face, her attraction remained strong to her long-time, but frustrating, love. "I was talking to him [Michael] while I was seeing Daniel, I didn't want to put all of my eggs in one basket."

Michael had grown up in Belford, N.J., one of the small fishing towns along Sandy Hook Bay, the son of a former Marine and a nurse. He also had a younger brother, Kevin, who had battled drug and alcohol problems and eventually died of a heart attack standing in line at a bank.

But this newest gentleman caller also displayed a warmth, honesty, and kindness that Cynthia had not seen in a prospective mate.

Cynthia agreed to a first date in the fall of 1995, remaining careful not to open up too much too quickly. She would not even let Michael pick her up at home, agreeing to meet him at a rest stop on the Garden State Parkway.

But that also allowed her to avoid introducing her parents and dealing with any third-degree they might give her new suitor. Assured he was no danger, Cynthia went with her date to a nearby night spot and ate and drank for several hours.

"We talked all night" she recalls with a smile. "I thought he was a great guy, he was so nice to me and he was such a nice person. I wasn't expecting anything, really. We took it slow and dated for a while."

Eventually, her biggest personal tragedy could not be avoided and she had to tell Michael about Carol, a revelation that would test both of them and force her to relive the sad past again.

"It was early on when you talk about your families. It came up that I didn't have any brothers or sisters so I had to tell him why," Cynthia said. "I never talked about her with anyone because it always felt so hopeless, I didn't know what to do with it all, but there was nowhere to go. I told him what had happened. When I told him they thought it was my father, he was kind of horrified by that."

But Michael showed his warmth and kindness and took the news as a comforting partner, not a frightened stranger. Ann and Frank came to support their relationship as well.

"My parents really liked Michael a lot, he did a lot of things for them," Cynthia said. "I was so done with them. I took care of them because they were old and Michael would help me."

But Michael moved quickly, proposing on New Year's Eve that year at his home in Middletown. "It was very nice and romantic. He got down on one knee."

The wedding would have to wait nearly four years, however, until December 1999. Michael's own life was baggage-filled as well. A tough divorce left him low on finances and with two teen children, a 12-year-old daughter and a 17-year-old son.

"He had children from another marriage and that is always a problem," said Cynthia. "We had a logistical problem because he lived with his mom and his daughter and he was really the caretaker of the family."

The couple moved in together in 1997, buying the small Middletown house Cynthia still occupies today. Since Michael had custody of his 12-year-old daughter, she came with him. The difficulties began as they would with any pre-teen forced to live with a new stepmother.

"He let her get away with anything she wanted to," Cynthia remembers, foreshadowing some later legal battles the two would engage in. Not long after, his 17-year-old son joined them after the boy's mother threw him out. But he didn't last long after being accused of stealing and disrespecting Cynthia, she said.

"I said to him, 'You have a mother, I don't need this.'" Cynthia recalls. Not long after that, Michael's daughter returned to her mother's home as well.

Eventually, their home life settled into a happy union and they tied the knot four days before Christmas, 1999, at the Middletown municipal building, married by then-mayor Raymond J. O'Grady.

Years later, O'Grady would be arrested and convicted of accepting bribes from undercover agents posing as contractors seeking government projects. His arrest was one of nearly two dozen involving public officials indicted as part of an FBI sting in Monmouth County.

In 2006, a jury took just three hours to find him guilty of all five counts of soliciting

Cynthia and Michael

and accepting $8,000 in bribes from undercover agents, according to *The New York Times*. He served 43 months in federal prison.

The investigation, dubbed Operation Bid Rig, was directed by then-United States Attorney and future Republican governor Chris Christie.

Cynthia finds their officiant's eventual downfall a funny side story, noting it did not hurt her marriage with Michael that would endure for more than 20 years.

"I was very happy with him, but we had to work so hard because he had to pay child support and all of that," she said. "I worked a lot and I was working all the time, he worked hard and never missed a day. I loved him very much, but I could never get over Daniel. He never knew about Daniel."

The wedding was somewhat bittersweet, coming just three weeks after Frank Farino's death from congestive heart failure.

The troubled father and husband never seemed to get over one daughter's brutal murder—and the lingering doubts by some about his rumored, but unproven involvement—and his inability to allow his surviving daughter to feel some of the support and love he could have given.

Frank had battled heart problems for years, likely increased by his smoking and a stressful approach to problems and family issues.

"He had it a long time before he died, he had to rest a lot," Cynthia recalls. "You get bloated and are not yourself and he got a little dementia after a while. And he wouldn't stop smoking, he smoked almost until the day he died."

That day was Dec. 4, 1999. His cremated remains are next to Carol at the same Gate of Heaven Cemetery in northern New Jersey. Ann Farino would live another 14 years, passing away on Memorial Day, 2015.

The couple is reunited in their final resting place as Cynthia placed her father's ashes in the same coffin as her mother.

Frank and Ann Farino

For the majority of their time together, Michael and Cynthia's relationship was a positive, loving union for two people who had been through difficult first marriages and found a way to rekindle something good.

"We had a good relationship," she recalled. "He was so sweet and nice. He always bought me flowers."

And he was there for her, never cheating or drinking, never any kind of abuse. He'd been through such things with previous women, as had Cynthia with her men, so each came to the coupling with a need for honest, proper treatment.

"We both worked a lot for a long time, he had child support to pay and his son wanted to go to college, so he footed the bill for that," Cynthia remembers. "[Michael's son] went and lasted two or three months and we had to pay off the loans."

Still, the duo shared good times while also taking care of an aging

Ann Farino. "We were working a lot and exhausted on the weekends, especially me," Cynthia says. "But we had a lot of good times."

Michael was an avid fisherman, but unlike some men who go off with the rod and reel and leave their wives behind, he would take Cynthia with him, even on trips to Key West, Florida, and elsewhere.

"He knew the places to get certain types of fishing." She recalled one year when they visited the Sea Bright Pier at night: "It was beautiful, he and I used to go on the party boats and you would fish all day. He would go and I would go with him for fun."

The couple also took advantage of the Jersey Shore eateries, often finding waterfront nightspots to try the best local seafood and Italian fare.

"He liked to eat out, we had a restaurant that was excellent," she said, citing Doris and Ed's of Highlands, which was knocked out by the tragic Hurricane Sandy. "It was gourmet dining at its best, you could see the water. It was nice and a great view of the bay."

July 4th was another favorite for Michael and Cynthia to dine al fresco as the rockets' red glared over the beach. "He loved Fourth of July."

But even better was when Michael would cook, along with tending to a major garden in their yard that had many varieties of tomatoes.

"We always had a big garden every summer, he grew a certain type of Italian squash," she said. "I let him take over the kitchen, I said, 'Knock yourself out.' He made a great pie crust and he made homemade pizza to die for," Cynthia recalls. "He made a Sicilian type pizza, it was amazing with this layering and no cheese."

Much of Michael's Italian food knowledge dated back to his childhood in neighboring Belford and the Valentino Family, which ran two pizzerias nearby and brought him in as a friend and longtime worker.

"They took him in and showed him how to make Italian food, and we would go over to their house, they knew how to do it," Cynthia said. "They would have us for all of the birthdays and their kids and grandkids. We would go to Christmas Eve at their house."

Brothers Ignazio and Enzo Valentino, who emigrated from Sicily in the 1960s, owned the pizzerias: Valentino's and Naples, both just a block apart in Belford. Since their passing, Naples was sold, but Valentino's continues to be run by one of their sons.

"They were not sure about me, but they came around because I was

Italian and they were great to me," she said. "We used to go play poker, they would have poker games twice a month. We saw quite a bit of them."

Gemma Valentino, Enzo's daughter and only child, recalls knowing Michael since his childhood and praised him as a great worker and family friend.

"Mike was respectful, kind, generous, and dependable, he was an amazing person. A great human being. I couldn't say enough nice things about him, I felt like he was a brother," Gemma said. "I remember him coming in a couple of nights a week and shredding the cheese, making dough, pizzeria prep and he knew how to make it. Mike was fun to work with, it was a pleasure knowing him."

When Cynthia came along, Gemma and her cousins, Ignazio's four boys, saw how she and Michael fit so well together.

"I met Cynthia when they were dating once or twice. I got to know her a lot more after my father passed away. We kept in touch for years. Michael would still do a lot of food prep for the pizzeria," Gemma said. "They were just a very good match. I loved to talk to the two of them very much."

"They would just laugh about things, they would laugh a lot. We would go to their house for dinner and reminisce and have a nice time with them. He loved to talk and shoot the shit and that was fun. There was never a dull moment."

Gemma was surprised when she eventually learned about Carol's murder because Cynthia did not seem like she dwelled on it or felt depressed or sorry for herself... another sign she was good at hiding the pain that remained with her since age 11.

"I remember when she told me about her sister, we went to her house to have dinner when she told me it was like someone had smacked me in the face," Gemma said. "I was stunned and tried not to cry. It was sad and disturbing at the same time."

"She only brought it up a couple of times, that is a pretty big deal. I never really brought it up, it would come up in conversation."

Cynthia did not want to burden people with her thoughts of Carol unless she felt they were willing to listen and offer support. Recalling bad memories of her father being a suspect and the family being treated differently by many neighbors and friends in Maplewood, the subject rarely came up.

But it was still uppermost in her mind and remains a mystery that never went away. "I used to talk to Audrey, my mom's caretaker, about it. I know my mother would have told her because she wanted people to feel sorry for her. She said I was right."

Still, Cynthia and Michael kept their marriage going strong most of the time, even with Ann's demands and his children's mixed reaction to Cynthia. "His son never stepped foot in the house, his daughter would come and visit, but she didn't appreciate anything. He loved them, but men do not have to be around their kids like women do."

Michael also became something of a hoarder, stocking up on groceries and canned goods to the point where she had dozens of them stacked in the basement after his death.

"He bought groceries all the time, I still have lots of booze that he kept and canned goods, groceries," Cynthia said. "He could be impractical, buying me things I didn't need. He didn't see that your house is the biggest investment and you have to take care of it."

But Michael also maintained a great work ethic, rising to the top of the technical service crew at Xerox, then later Global Imaging, which put him in charge of training others. "He was so good with computers that they put him on training. He was a very bright person." With Cynthia's cleaning business going, the money came in handy. "I was making good money, but everything went to the household bills."

When Hurricane Sandy hit on Oct. 29, 2012, it was one of the worst natural disasters in New Jersey history and the largest recorded hurricane in the Atlantic Ocean at the time.

Michael and Cynthia were in the thick of it, losing power for weeks and fighting a bitter fall chill for days.

"We lost power for a long time, and it was getting cold. We had a generator, but it needed a part. We had to go all the way to Hunterdon County to get a generator," she said. "The electricity came back on after almost a month. We were desperate."

She said their small house just blocks from the water did not suffer severe damage, but the neighborhood was torn apart.

"I wasn't able to work because all of my clients were in this area and out of power," she said. "Michael was able to go to work, but not for a few days."

Being stuck together in the house for weeks turned out to be a blessing, she said, as they grew closer and closer together.

"We did everything together anyway, we had no problem being together all of the time, we were very close," Cynthia recalls. "We were trying to keep the cat warm and I like to read so I wasn't so crazed as he was, he could not use his computer."

When 2014 came along, things started to get grim, with a string of health issues affecting the family. First, Ann Farino took a turn for the worse and ended up in the hospital, forcing Cynthia to give up the cleaning business and tend to her full-time.

"She was in and out of the hospital a lot to the point where I couldn't keep taking care of her house and seeing her," she said. "We had someone move in to help her near the end."

By late May 2015, Ann Farino was dead, passing away at home and joining her husband and oldest daughter at Gate of Heaven Cemetery. She was 96.

Just weeks later, Cynthia had her own medical run-in when an incarcerated hernia woke her up in the middle of the night with nausea and vomiting. "I woke Michael up and I went to the emergency room and was in a great deal of pain." The condition kept her there for days, eventually turning into a week because of a major blizzard that blocked access.

The worst news came a year later when Michael was diagnosed with pancreatic cancer. This handsome, rugged, and healthy man was struck down like a feeble child.

"He did very well in the beginning, and they thought he was in remission it but it started growing again," Cynthia recalled. "Our whole lives revolved around going to Sloan Kettering and taking care of his cancer. My whole life kind of stopped then, I had to stay home and be with him."

The American Cancer Society estimates about 57,600 people, mostly men, are diagnosed with pancreatic cancer each year, while 47,050 people die of it. The odds were not good.

And then there was the chemotherapy, which helped reduce the spread, but had nasty side effects. "Chemo is chemo, but it does such awful things to the rest of you, so we had to counteract that. We did a lot of homeopathic things," Cynthia said. "A lot of herbals and things that boost your immune system. He would drink a tea that was good for him. Cancer is simple, it is an inflamed area so you need to take stuff that boosts your immunity and is anti-inflammatory."

At one point, Michael was responding to the treatments and his blood-work and other tests showed major improvement. But by early 2020, he was in rough shape and ended up in Riverview Medical Center in nearby Red Bank. "He was in and out the last months of his life, he was going in and out for a lot of things," Cynthia said.

Then when Covid-19 hit in March of that year, Michael could not have visitors, not even his wife.

"They wouldn't let me visit him because of Covid and he didn't want to stay in the hospital, they weren't doing anything at this point," she said. "We wanted him discharged and have hospice at home, I didn't want him to die alone. He was home for three weeks before he died. "

Michael passed away in the home he loved with the woman he loved on May 15, 2020. He is buried in Memorial Park in Tinton Falls, just down the Parkway from their house.

"Because of Covid we were allowed five or six people at the wake and only four or five at the cemetery," Cynthia said. "It was pretty bad, it was pretty dreary."

That final goodbye brought up all of the sadness Cynthia had endured: losing her mother just a few years earlier, her dysfunctional father 15 years before that, and, of course, her sister, gone more than 50 years.

"I was so devastated and stressed out and aggravated. I didn't want to even think of her," Cynthia recalls. "When people die, it brings up everything I don't want to think about, my whole life has changed, it is just stressful."

But it also reminded her how much she needed to find out about Carol's death, how she died, and who could have done it. Cynthia remained adamant that the Maplewood Police and the Essex County Prosecutor's Office had not done enough, and that answers were still out there waiting to be uncovered, even if those in law enforcement did not want to provide them.

Some might say it is a long shot. But after surviving troubled relationships, dysfunctional parents, and a string of other personal issues, Cynthia was ready to go after the biggest challenge yet: Justice.

Chapter Fifteen

I first approached Cynthia Farino in early April of 2020.

At that time, her husband, Michael, was still alive but in the final difficulties of his illness. He was friendly and kind when he answered the phone the first time I called, then handed me over to Cynthia.

She seemed surprised that I wanted to look into the case of her sister's death, but initially was pleased that someone was trying to find the truth, or at least tell the story.

However, she also said it was not the right time as Michael needed her attention, understandably so. I went on to other interviews for the book.

I'd been researching Carol's death for several months and had found many former friends and a handful of news clippings, as well as some police accounts that helped my efforts.

Still, the official law enforcement response from Maplewood Police and the Essex County Prosecutor's Office was limited.

It would soon get worse.

As a longtime Maplewood resident and former editor of a website that covered the township, I had always had good relations with the cops. Keeping the police radio scanner on most days as I worked, I could hear everything that went on among the patrols and never found instances of improper or biased behavior.

There was one time that I was recording video on my phone as police arrested an apparent robbery suspect outside of a liquor store one day. When one of the officers saw me, he ordered me to stop recording, which is a violation of my rights, and eventually grabbed my camera phone from me.

When I promised to stop recording he gave it back. I reported his violation to the police, they investigated but punished him only with an order to receive some kind of additional training—or so I was told.

Still, my requests for police department public information through the federal Freedom of Information Act (FOIA) or the state's version, the Open Public Records Act (OPRA) were often granted with no problems. I even recall getting CD recordings of dramatic 911 calls within hours of requests in some cases.

So when I went looking for the data and files on the 54-year-old Carol Ann Farino case in February 2020, I was surprised at the roadblock they put up. My initial request resulted in the first police reports from the night she was murdered and a copy of the letter the police chief sent to Michigan authorities in 1969 about similar murders there, which I covered in an earlier chapter.

But nothing further.

Maplewood Police delayed the effort with initial emails saying the files needed to be reviewed to make sure that nothing that could hinder the investigation was going to be released.

When the Covid-19 pandemic hit in March 2020, the cops claimed that was taking their time with manpower issues and trying to increase safety efforts for officers on patrol, as well as the public.

Police Chief Jimmy DeVaul, who had indicated a willingness to consider releasing more information, also revealed that Covid-19 was causing problems even in his personal life. In a May 8, 2020 email he revealed that his own mother had passed away from the virus that week.

> Sir,
> I am not going to lie...my mother died on Sunday because of Covid19... The department has been dealing with the stress surrounding the circumstances. I have not even looked at the files.... the timing has just been bad. I promise we will talk soon as things stabilize.
> Thank you for understanding.
> Chief

I responded with condolences and realized it was not a good time to be seeking information from that source.

DeVaul, who had been chief for only two years, had also taken over at a difficult time for the local police.

Former Police Chief Robert Cimino and one of his captains had been forced out of the department in 2017 after an incident in which officers were accused of forcing people of color out of town and abusing others.

The clashes occurred on July 5, 2016, after the annual fireworks display. Due to rain on July 4, the show had been delayed a day. Because of the delay, officials allowed anyone to attend inside the fenced-in area that had been previously been limited to those purchasing $10 tickets.

The reasoning: some tickets had already been collected and forcing those residents to pay again would not have been fair. But the practice meant larger crowds would attend the July 5 fireworks event.

When the display show ended, larger crowds began walking north toward South Orange, with some ending up in fights or other disturbances.

As police tried to break them up, some received an order to usher crowds to the South Orange or neighboring Irvington line, including many who said they lived in Maplewood—nearly all of them non-white. There were also claims of police abuse and at least one video clip of an officer holding down a youth and kicking him.

Maplewood Police later hired an outside investigator to review the incidents while the Essex County Prosecutor's Office did its own investigation but ended up finding no evidence of wrongdoing.

But the township review, which was never released, apparently found enough evidence to prompt the Township Committee in August 2017 to put veteran Police Chief Robert Cimino and a police captain on leave and vote unanimously to request their resignations.

Less than two months later, a buyout for nearly $280,000 was arranged with the chief that also included letters of recommendation that drew some criticism as part of a deal for him to resign.

Township officials said the state process for removing a police chief that they claimed would have required charging him with a criminal offense and paying legal fees to go to court would have cost more.

Once Cimino was gone, DeVaul had taken over as interim chief in August 2017 and became the permanent top cop in April 2018. In his time, he had received good marks for getting the department past the July 5 uproar and forced police chief retirement.

But things were far from perfect as claims of racial inequality still occurred. A 2019 special report from *The Star-Ledger* revealed Maplewood Police had the highest rate of "use of force" incidents in New Jersey.

It found that Maplewood cops used force in more than 11 percent of arrests from 2012 to 2016, "more than three times the state average—and also applied force disproportionately on black people and, in particular, black youths." Use of force means either physical altercations such as strong-arm holds, kicking, punching, or hitting, or use of outside items such as pepper spray, stun guns, or firearms.

After completing other elements of research, I touched base with Chief DeVaul again via email on July 3, 2020, nearly two months after my initial contact. He responded three days later that he had assigned Detective Christopher Dolias to help with my research.

Dolias reached out nearly a month later, with initial indications that he would help, saying via email:

> I want to apologize for taking so long to get back to you as I was out of the office since last week. Thank you for reaching out to me about this case and if you are available to talk at some point that would be great. I do want to let you know I am in the process of reading through the investigations into the case and due to my current position I unfortunately cannot dedicate my full day to it.
>
> I expect to be done reading through what I have in the next week or so. With that being said, because it is still an active investigation I can't share more than you have received in your last OPRA request as far as documents.
>
> What I am hoping though is for input from you on the research you have already done and if you have questions for me I will gladly answer what I can and if I don't have an answer at this moment I will see what I can find out.
>
> Prior to me speaking with Carol's sister I would be very interested to hear what information she has provided you and any other details you have come across.

That seemed a bit arrogant, to say that police information would be limited, but he wanted to know what Cynthia and I had found for their use. But I remained willing to do whatever would work.

I had finally touched base again with Cynthia in July, two months after her husband's death. She thanked me for my condolences and said she was ready to help with the research and hopefully a path to solving her 54-year-old nightmare mystery.

I interviewed her several times over the following weeks, which resulted in great insight on her family and the case, as well as lists of potential sources and background. Much of that information you have already read in previous pages.

On August 28, 2020, I heard again from Detective Dolias, who made arrangements to chat later that week. After we chatted, he said that I could arrange to come in and go through what he said was an inch-thick file of information on Carol's case under his supervision and without any copies being made. I agreed and emailed Chief DeVaul and Det. Dolias on September 2 about this, adding that Cynthia was interested in seeing the files as well.

The chief's response to me and Dolias, in part:

I take no issue in having the both of you review the file without releasing any documents. If you want copies of reports, I may ask for an official OPRA request at some point.

However before I release anything I would need to consult with the Essex County prosecutor's office who may still retain jurisdiction. Give them a chance to object or not.

Our Twp. Attorney may want some sort of hold harmless agreement???

Det. Dolias please let me know how much time you will need to review the entire file... I don't like surprises.

Thank you both.

Chief

That was the first hint that access could be denied and that the prosecutor's office would likely be the chief blockade. Still, I went forth with Dolias in planning a review.

I emailed the detective that I would also like to see what evidence remains, such as Carol's uniform, other clothes, and the stocking used to strangle her. Cynthia had also mentioned that a necklace Carol wore and recordings of her interview with detectives at the time that she was told were lost.

His response in a Sept 8, 2020, email:

I hope you enjoyed your Labor Day weekend. Unfortunately I don't have access to the evidence locker this week as the main Evidence Detective is out the remainder of the week so I cannot give you an answer on the necklace and don't want to speculate without putting eyes on it. As for a recording of her sister's interview it would as well be in the locker if we have it so that's the same as the necklace.

I think it would be best if we set a 4-hour block I can sit with you as you go through the files and set additional time as needed to get a look at it all and understand the work already done would probably be around 8 at least. Chief if you [are] fine with it I can make arrangements with Joe on when this is done.

[Editor's Note: It was a ring that was missing, not a necklace]

Things were looking good as Dolias later mentioned Oct. 3, 2020, as a possible day for our sit-down in a follow-up email:

I spoke with Chief DeVaul and him [sic] and I plan on taking a look at the files on Thursday so once that happens I should have a better idea on when we can set up time for you to come and take a look. I know you said weekends are best but the next free day I have on a Saturday won't be until Oct. 3rd. If you wanted to take a look before that I can definitely stay late a night or two during the week before that.

In a Sept. 22 email, Dolias confirmed that 8 a.m. on October 3 would be the date for us to review the file and possible evidence.

I cleared my calendar.

Then, three days before our planned review, the bottom fell out.

Dolias emailed the following:

The Chief and I had a chance to go through the case file today and this time we feel that due to the amount of information we are going through it would not be responsible of us to have you come look at the case file this weekend before we can really understand all the work that was done and what our exact next steps are. I look forward to speaking to you more when the time is appropriate in our case and I will be reaching out in the future. I apologize about the short notice.

That was the last I heard from either of them despite several efforts to reach out and set up a new meeting to at least discuss how we could proceed. I strongly suspected that the police were blocked from sharing anything by The Essex County Prosecutor's Office.

As former detective John Perna had advised me earlier, the county investigators had the final say on any investigations involving felony or high-profile serious crimes, especially murder.

No surprise, then, that when Dolias or DeVaul likely sought permission from the county to re-open and/or offer some of the files to me for review they were shut down.

Cynthia had filed her own request for access to the files in a September 9 FOIA request to Maplewood Police, in which she explained who she was in relation to Carol. She first received a notice that it would take the department an additional 21 days to review. But it also added, "We are seeking further clarification from the Essex County Prosecutor's Office."

Cynthia responded to the Maplewood Police with a note indicating she had reached out to the prosecutor's office and received a blunt message that they had no such records, without an explanation of whether that meant no records at all or none they would share with the victim's sister.

Chief DeVaul got into the discussion, even mentioning me, by emailing Cynthia on Oct. 27 the following:

> Our records reflect that basic information related to the incident has previously been provided to Mr. Strupp. I can provide the same information if you would like. Certain information, such as criminal investigatory records are listed as an exemption under OPRA.
>
> This is an unsolved case. Further, the investigating jurisdiction of this incident would be the Essex County Prosecutor's office Major Crimes division. We would not release any information of this nature without their authority. We are coordinating this effort on your behalf and will determine who the appropriate contact person would be.
>
> We will keep you updated as information is developed as to your request. I have copied Det. Plesnik on this email who will be coordinating our efforts with ECPO.

When Cynthia responded on Oct. 28, 2020, with a terse letter noting she deserved better treatment as the only remaining survivor of the family, no further response was received.

The next step would be the Essex County Prosecutor's Office, which would turn out to be worse.

Before approaching Maplewood Police, I had earlier filed an OPRA request with the prosecutor's office in February 2020, but to no avail.

Unlike DeVaul, who at least seemed willing to help initially, the Essex County Prosecutor's Office sent me a five-page email detailing why they did not have to help me and claiming the case was still under investigation.

Even though it was more than 50 years old and there had been no signs of the Prosecutor's Office making any new inquiries or finding any new clues or evidence, they hid behind that catch-all "under investigation" claim.

Despite my request clearly stating that I wanted to see "all records, documents, interviews, and correspondence" related to the investigation of Carol's murder, they called it too broad. Most reporter OPRA requests are worded that way so as to encompass everything.

The bureaucratic letter from Assistant Prosecutor Stephen Pogany also cited a string of cases that apparently allowed them to keep the information from me due to the fact that it is an investigatory record and not, apparently, subject to disclosure.

Finally, it claimed that the prosecutor's office did not have to go through records to see which could be released and which could not. Also untrue. I have received plenty of past records that have redacted information.

It made clear the prosecutor's office had no intention of providing help to our investigation and showed no signs of expanding their own. Was this an effort to hide what had been poorly done in the past on this case or just laziness at not wanting to do something that might help to solve it?

The Essex County Prosecutor's Office does not have a stellar record in many areas.

As I had noted previously, my first entanglement with them came 20 years earlier after the murder of another Maplewood resident, Christine Burns. The divorced teacher and mother of two was brutally attacked and stabbed to death in her home on December 8, 2000.

When I began looking into it for a 2003 *New Jersey Monthly* story, I discovered that a man had been arrested for an attempted sexual assault of a woman just five blocks from Burns's home five months after her death.

I asked prosecutors if they had ever sought to test his DNA to see if it matched what was at the murder scene and they claimed they never even tried. They could have asked for a court order to collect his DNA but told me they did not think it would have worked.

Is that how you run an investigation? Decide if something will work before you try?

In the end, a state law was passed requiring that anyone convicted of certain felonies have their DNA tested against the state DNA database. They were forced to do so and it matched. The man, 28-year-old Douglas Manning, never even went to trial, pleading guilty to a charge of aggravated manslaughter and aggravated sexual assault in a deal that sent him to prison for 20 years.

The prosecutor's office, which dates back to 1829, has had other issues. Aside from an ongoing lack of staff to handle the large number of cases out of crime spots like Newark, Irvington, and related areas, it has had its share of big case goofs.

One of the most well-known was also in Maplewood—the Wee Care Nursery School case, which targeted a pre-school in St. George's Church on Ridgewood Avenue.

In 1985, Wee Care aide Kelly Michaels was arrested on allegations of sexually abusing children after one youngster told a nurse he had been given a rectal examination at the school. The Essex County Prosecutor's Office joined the police investigation that led to an indictment against Michaels.

She was convicted and sentenced to 47 years in jail when prosecutors claimed 51 students had been molested. But it would later be revealed that students were coerced and investigators used leading questions on the young witnesses that all but forced them to agree that illegal acts occurred that had not even been mentioned by the children.

After five years in prison, Michaels was released when a state appeals court overturned the case, finding that it was tainted by unreliable and inadmissible expert testimony. The ruling stated that a prosecution expert "was permitted to lead the jury to believe that the [interviewing] process was rooted in science and thus was a reliable means of determining sex abuse."

The New Jersey state Supreme Court later upheld that decision, ruling "the interrogations that occurred in this case were improper and there is substantial likelihood that the evidence derived from them is unreliable."

The investigative blunder became a textbook example of prosecutorial overreach, prompting the *Los Angeles Times* to state it was part of a "horrifying phenomenon of the 1980s, in which reports of mass child abuse became common just as a generation of parents came to rely on day-care workers to watch over their toddlers and preschoolers."

The Wall Street Journal's Pulitzer Prize-winning columnist Dorothy Rabinowitz helped bring about a re-examination of the case during her time at Harper's magazine in the early 1990s. She also examined it as one of several cases in her 2004 book, *No Crueler Tyrannies: Accusation, False Witnesses and Other Terrors of Our Times.*

In a 1993 *Journal* piece, she wrote that "the children had been bribed, bullied, begged and betrayed so that they would, after endless hours of insistent questioning, finally say that Kelly Michaels had done this or that to them."

In 1999, the prosecutor's office—then headed by Patricia A. Hurt—came under fire for overreaching its investigation of the shooting death of a police officer, which included alleged beatings of suspects.

Hurt was also accused of misuse of power ranging from "wasting tax-payers' money on luxury office appointments, like a $120 leather waste-basket, and unjustified salary increases" to "some current and former employees... suing her for what they contend was age and gender discrimination when Hurt made promotions," according to *The New York Times.*

The major criticism related to her office's handling of the April 8, 1999, killing of Orange Police Officer Joyce Carnegie, who was shot as she sought to arrest a suspect in a series of robberies.

"The killing of the 38-year-old officer set off a frenetic effort to track down her assailant—one fraught with confusion and, in the eyes of some law enforcement officials, gross incompetence," *The Star-Ledger* wrote in 2009. "Before the killer was safely behind bars, innocent men had been rounded up, one of them beaten and killed by Carnegie's fellow officers. The bungled investigation marked the beginning of a slow, evolutionary change that forced out… Hurt and forever changed the office."

Then there was the January 2000 dormitory fire in Seton Hall University's Boland Hall in South Orange, next to Maplewood. The tragedy, which began as a prank when two students set a banner on fire in a lounge area, ended with the deaths of three students and injuries to 58 others.

The Essex County Prosecutor's Office did not obtain indictments of the two students, Joseph LePore and Sean Ryan, until 2003, prompting criticism for delays.

When the two suspects eventually agreed to a plea deal on lesser charges of arson and witness tampering instead of murder, and received only five years in prison each, then-County Prosecutor Paula Dow took criticism. Her office also dropped efforts to charge one of the guilty student's parents, sister, and friend who had helped cover up the crime.

Dow had been appointed earlier that year by then-Governor James McGreevey, a Democrat who would later resign after revealing he was gay and had appointed a lover to a sensitive homeland security post.

Dow, who happens to live in Maplewood, would serve until December 2009, when Governor Chris Christie appointed her to be state attorney general. She held that job until 2011 and became a state Superior Court judge in 2012, a post she still holds.

Since Dow left, the Essex County Prosecutor's Office has been overseen by three different county prosecutors over nine years.

Robert Laurino, who had been with the office as a prosecutor since 1980, took over in December 2009 as acting Essex County Prosecutor when Dow left. He served until Feb. 22, 2011, when Carolyn Murray was sworn in as Acting Essex County Prosecutor.

Murray left to become a state Superior Court judge in May 2017, prompting the re-appointment of Laurino again as acting county prosecutor. He served in that temporary role until Sept. 4, 2018, when Gov. Phil Murphy chose Theodore N. Stephens to be acting Essex County Prosecutor, a post he has held ever since.

The last inquiry I made for information on the Farino case in December 2020 brought this response from a county prosecutor spokesperson: "We are reviewing the case. Homicide cases are never closed unless there is an arrest or some other resolution."

When asked for further details on what that entailed, nothing was provided.

For the major law enforcement agencies responsible for solving the murder of Carol Ann Farino to essentially slam the door on her only surviving relative, and at the same time ask her to give them information, seems both rude and offensive.

Cynthia Farino lost a sister and, later, both parents, while living with the emptiness that such a tragedy can bring—and from age 11. Meanwhile, the Essex County Prosecutor's Office, which has offered no proof of any kind of continuing its inquiries, throws around the claim of "active investigation" like a church cites its religious institution moniker to avoid paying taxes.

Cynthia has made it clear that her family has received barely any contact from either the prosecutor's office or the Maplewood Police in more than 30 years. One would think a real effort to put this mystery to bed would include a new outreach.

But Cynthia has not given up and at the time this book went to press had been in talks with attorneys to find a way in court to force access to the "inch-thick" file Maplewood Police had mentioned. If it is truly out of their hands to allow a real re-opening of the case without the county prosecutor's blessing, that is also a backward approach to law enforcement.

One attorney had cited the possibility of "common law right of access," which would allow Cynthia to see the files as the closest living relative who has a right to see how it was handled or mishandled.

There are precedents in allowing documents ordinarily protected by investigative agencies to be released as common law items.

Most recently, *The Asbury Park Press* was granted access to a former Neptune, N.J. police officer's internal files after he was convicted of shooting his ex-wife in front of their seven-year-old daughter in 2015. (Full disclosure: I have been a *Press* reporter since May 2019).

But the access occurred after a three-year court battle that the newspaper waged to gain access to the files of former Neptune police Sgt. Philip Seidle, who killed Tamara Wilson-Seidle in the incident.

State Attorney General S. Gurbir Grewal had blocked the release of the files as recently as June 2020, but decided to release the information in December 2020, stating "I hope that these disclosures, which build on the information and records already in the public domain, will shine a light on this matter and inform the debate over what, if any, changes are necessary to avoid such tragic incidents in the future."

Essentially, the law states that the interest of a person seeking access, such as Cynthia, must outweigh the law enforcement agencies' interest in keeping it confidential. One could argue that a case that has seen no real progress in 50 years would not be harmed by the one lone surviving relative of the victim finding out what has been done so far to solve it.

But without the extended files, it is not hard to determine the most likely suspect. Someone who was later accused of a similar murder, someone who worked and, for a time lived, in Maplewood Village just a block from Carol Farino's last known location, and someone who died in a mental hospital after being sent there following a violent incident in public.

That someone is Otto Neil Nilson.

Along with all of those pieces of evidence, or at least speculation, Cynthia Farino recalls her sister talking about a friendly, strange man who would come into the restaurant where she worked and discuss religion.

"She came home and said she met this very nice man who worked across the street and would talk to her," Cynthia recalls, later realizing it was Nilson. "But we did not know until later what kind of man he was."

But Cynthia did eventually find someone who would add a very strong piece of the puzzle that Nilson had killed her sister. Someone outside of law enforcement, but with a very strong record of helping those inside.

Chapter Sixteen

As law enforcement refused to offer any more information on what they have been doing on the Carol Ann Farino case for the past 50-plus years—or more likely, not doing—Cynthia Farino would not give up.

Among the positive results of our renewed interest in the case was my contacting two of Cynthia's former closest friends from the past: Gabe and Angela.

As noted earlier, Gabe had met Cynthia at Fielding School, while Angela has known her since seventh grade.

After I reached out to them for comments and information, Cynthia renewed her friendship with both, spending wonderful nights and afternoons visiting, sharing drinks, and talking over old times during much of 2020.

And, of course, chatting about Carol's death and what might have occurred.

At one point, Angela passed along Carol's photo to a friend who worked as a medium and had specialized in breaking cold cases and other serious crimes, especially murders.

This was not the woman mentioned earlier in Northern New Jersey who held a lengthy, but mixed-success session with Cynthia in her home.

Angela's friend was Queens-based clairvoyant Maggie Remigio, 57, a former bank officer and construction company owner with strong ties and success in helping law enforcement crack some of the most high-profile cases of the past few decades.

"She's never wrong," famed New York defense attorney James Lenihan said about her. "She has sat with me for jury selection and helped me pick a jury in a sex abuse case. She knew what to do."

Maggie says Carol Ann Farino's killer was Otto Neil Nilson.

"She said that's him," Angela Caruso recalls about Maggie's reaction to seeing Nilson's photo the first time. "That's the man that did it to her."

Angela, who operates a salon in Essex County, N.J., first met Maggie in 2008 when one of her hair clients and friends suggested using the medium for a reading. Skeptical, she went into the experience with at least some curiosity.

Just moments after sitting down with her, Maggie knew that Angela's deceased father's name was Joseph and her parents were in a variety show in their retirement home. She even knew the song they used to sing: "Let Me Call You Sweetheart."

"There was no way, no way she would know that," Angela recalled. "It was so real. Even my friend whose house I went to didn't know about that song and didn't know my father's name. This was too ironically real, there was not anything I did not believe."

They've been in touch daily ever since.

"If I have something on my mind, to sell my business or something, I would go to her for a reading and we go through it," Angela explains. "Or if it was something with my son. She predicted my business would be moving and move again and it happened."

Maggie, a Cuban native, said the unique ability hit her as a 4-year-old on a Havana street when she saw a young boy hit by a car. As people ran to help him she recalled an image of him rising and waving goodbye.

When her family fled Castro's rule, Maggie's father claimed political asylum, later penning a book on his experience as a paramedic during the Bay of Pigs invasion, titled 60 to 1.

"I came from a very upscale family in Cuba, they were very affluent people," Maggie said. "But that means nothing in a communist country."

Maggie's family eventually lived in New York, Florida, and New Jersey, before settling in Queens in 2018. Married twice, she has two daughters and four grandchildren.

Skeptics may disagree with Maggie's efforts and insight, and they have a right to do so. Thousands of so-called mediums set up shop nationwide with false claims as they rip off client after client with exaggerated assertions.

But in law enforcement and the hunt for unknown assailants, especially murderers, history is filled with mediums, psychics, and hypnotists used to glean information. In the early days of Carol's investigation, as previously noted, Maplewood Police utilized a psychic and several hypnotism sessions.

"You rarely hear of law enforcement praising a psychic for helping to solve a crime, and psychics are rarely used in police investigations, at least in any official capacity," a 2020 *Reader's Digest* article stated. "…That doesn't mean, however, that there aren't cases in which psychics have played an important role, either in helping to identify new evidence or in confirming detectives are on the right track."

The same article cited 20 such cases dating back decades, including several in New Jersey that were aided in their work by legitimate clairvoyants: "[l]egitimate psychics exist and have actually played an important role in solving a select group of crimes and other mysteries."

Among those noted in the piece was the 1982 murder of 18-year-old Amie Hoffman of Morristown, N.J., who was last seen leaving her job at a nearby mall.

When police were unable to find Hoffman or her killer, they reached out to Nancy Weber, a local psychic they'd successfully used in the past, *Reader's Digest* said. "Nancy, who had already had visions of Hoffman's body and the assault she had endured before being killed, led police down an investigative trail that ultimately ended with the murder conviction of James Koedatich."

Maggie's record of success convinced Lenihan and Angela to believe years ago, while drawing Cynthia's curiosity enough to take it seriously, especially given so much other speculation on Nilson's potential guilt.

"Everything she has told me is true about witnesses, what they were going to do, what they were going to say, and what to be ready for," Lenihan said about Maggie. "I trust her."

Lenihan is no slouch. He's known for a string of high-profile defense clients, including the infamous "Fatal Attraction" killer Carolyn Warmus, who was convicted of shooting her lover's wife, Betty Jeanne Solomon, nine times in 1989.

She was sentenced to 25 years to life in prison and later sued her previous defense attorney, Julia Heit, for allegedly botching her case.

The killing sparked two TV movies at the time and comparisons to the 1987 movie thriller, *Fatal Attraction*, in which Michael Douglas portrays a married man who has an affair with Glenn Close's character that leads to stalking and near-murder.

Lenihan represented Warmus in her 2017 lawsuit, claiming her side was not properly presented at trial. The case sparked a CNN hour-long special that year that highlighted Lenihan's work.

The attorney was also on the defense team of Saul Dos Reis, a 25-year-old Danbury, Connecticut man who was accused of killing a 13-year-old girl he met on the Internet in 2002.

Dos Reis said the killing was accidental during "rough sex" in a McDonald's parking lot outside of a Danbury mall. He was eventually sentenced to 25 years in prison. Lenihan appealed and claimed that the girl actually died from a heart condition and possibly related to an orgasm at the time of her death.

That case also drew widespread national attention from the likes of the *Los Angeles Times*, CNN, and *60 Minutes II*.

So with such a respectable and high-profile reputation, Lenihan has no reason to support a medium whose work draws skeptics and could impact his livelihood unless he is 100% behind her.

He said his support for Maggie's work dates back to 2008 when she convinced him she had been in contact with the girl killed in the Danbury case, 13-year-old Christina Long. As Lenihan walked out of his office, he passed an outdoor cafe where a friend of a client, named Paul, was sitting and speaking to Maggie on his cell phone.

"He saw me walk by and asked where I was going," Lenihan said. "I said I was going to court. Then he said, 'This is for you, just listen' and handed me the phone."

When Lenihan put his ear to the phone, he heard Maggie's voice for the first time. She told him that the second she overheard Lenihan speak to Paul, Long reached out to her and began to make contact.

"She said 'You're a fucking asshole,'" Maggie told him. He said, "Really?" Both offended and curious, Lenihan inquired further with this sudden new acquaintance.

Maggie told him she was a medium and the girl who had contacted her was named Christina. She asked Lenihan if he knew her. He said he had represented a man accused of killing a Christina.

Then it made sense to both why Christina was mad at him.

And it launched a relationship that has seen Maggie help Lenihan with at least 15 cases over the years, some she knew about before he did.

"What she does is she will tell me that someone is going to come in my office about a case and that it is true and I have to help this case," Lenihan explains. "The majority of times that she calls me it is someone that I have to help, and she is always right."

He cited an attempted murder case in which Lenihan was acting as defense attorney for the accused: "She told me that my client didn't do it and I had to defend him." She also knew the accused's name after it came to her before there was any publicity. The defendant was acquitted.

There was also the time that Maggie predicted a would-be client would come to Lenihan's office the next day and offer "a bag of money" to represent him.

"No matter what, you can't even touch that money," she told him. "If you do you will wind up getting arrested because this is a bad man." Lenihan said it happened as she predicted, he turned him down and later found out about his questionable past.

As far as Lenihan is concerned, anything Maggie says about Nilson being Carol's killer is to be believed: "If she says this is the guy who did it, in my book, he is the guy who did it."

So if he's willing to take her word as fact, it's not surprising those involved in Carol's case would also.

"I think I trust her judgment," Cynthia said about Maggie's definitive claims that Otto Nilson killed her sister. "It makes the most sense, he

[Nilson] had access to her constantly. He knew how she walked home and when she didn't get a ride because he was probably stalking her."

Maggie's role in the case came about shortly after I first connected with Cynthia in the Summer of 2020. After the first of numerous interviews with Carol's sister, I sought to speak with people she and Carol knew back in their Maplewood days.

Angela and Gabe were tops on Cynthia's list.

After talking with me a few times, both rekindled their relationships with Cynthia, resulting in many phone calls and in-person gatherings among the threesome. During one such encounter at Angela's northern New Jersey home, I joined in via Zoom.

Then Angela got the idea to tap Maggie's expertise given her history with cold case murders and criminal investigations. She had not only helped Lenihan in the past, but other private investigators as well.

"I feel like I am called to do this, it's an inherited thing," said Maggie, a Cuban native who came to the United States with her parents in 1968 as a five-year-old. "It's a way of life."

Angela first contacted Maggie about Carol's murder in October 2020 and sent a picture of Carol to Maggie, but offered no other details of her death.

"As soon as she saw it that was the beginning of all of it," Angela said. "She got inundated with [mental images] and she knew [Carol] was strangled and she was with her, her thoughts of her were in her mind for weeks."

Cynthia Farino was unaware of this at the time but was soon pulled in when Maggie called her and began telling her who she was, how she knew about her, and that Carol had been in touch.

"I had no idea they were going to do this," Cynthia said about Angela and Maggie. "The first time she called out of the blue. I did not even answer when I saw the number because I did not recognize it, so Maggie called back."

They ended up talking by phone several times and each call brought more information about Carol and her murder that Maggie could not have known and that Angela would not have known either to tell her.

When she mentioned Otto Nilson and described him, Cynthia be-

Joe Strupp

came more and more convinced: "I have a feeling that she is probably right; logically it makes the most sense. We thought it was him all along, but I would like some concrete evidence."

But Maggie was not finished and would receive images and messages purportedly from Carol telling her that this man had done it and she wanted to have some closure.

"When I saw the picture of this girl it was like floodgates, a lot of things with the case are an act of passion, the person that killed her knew of her, it was not somebody who just met her, there was a connection, an emotional connection," Maggie said in an interview. "I see this person visiting a coffee shop, I see this young lady tending to this man, I see that this man was served coffee from this lady."

That led to a possible connection as Nilson was considered a semi-regular visitor to Milt's Cup & Saucer, where Carol worked. He also worked across the street from the eatery at the time.

"This sister was very sweet, she was not the type to turn people down, she was one to gab with everyone, even the most undesirable," Maggie added. "The strong feeling is it was a serial killer. This was a man who knew this girl, who had seen her often and was served by her. I see a man who carried a newspaper underneath his arm, well dressed and kind of dorky with short sleeves."

Maggie described the killer as someone needing women as a form of support, a loner and recluse who also showed some remorse for what he had done. Police indicated that Carol's body was left in its final spot on Hubert Place carefully, almost with reverence rather than being tossed out the door as his car passed by.

"The way he left her is that it shows a bit of remorse, it is almost like, 'are you okay,'" she said. "He had killed other people and DNA would prove a connection. I believe that this case is connected to other cases and they could say that it is connected to other cases in a five-mile radius."

She even went on to cite Nilson's possible past as a victim of sexual abuse or a purveyor of it: "He had secrets, he might be a victim of child molestation, there are relationship issues with women, the life cycle of him was a lot of darkness and secrets."

Nilson's later arrest for a similar crime would help support that claim, along with his eventual sentencing to psychiatric care after attacking people in the veterans' hospital.

"There was a lot of rage," Maggie said about Carol's killer. "He had a sexual dysfunction."

Then Maggie went after investigators: "That police department totally botched this case, I see a lot of investigation, but I don't see questions. They did not go far, the police didn't do their job and they let it go."

Maggie would go on to receive what she claimed were images and messages from Carol through the fall of 2020, all of which sought closure to the case and Carol's need to be "at rest."

"It opened up the floodgates and it went on and on and on," Maggie explained. "It lured me in for weeks."

Each time she called Angela and asked her to meet her or let her visit New Jersey and spend time with her friend to try to clear it up. "It became an almost daily conversation," Angela said. "She kept getting these pictures of Carol [in her mind] and felt the need to bring her somewhere."

Maggie would call Angela without notice and begin to even speak as though she was speaking for Carol, saying words that she said came through her from the deceased girl.

"I'd see pictures and images and feeling like I lived there," Maggie said. "Lots of names and there was more to the story."

By early December 2020, it came to a head during two emotional incidents that had Maggie reach a level of connection she had not experienced in many years and what she believes brought Carol some peace.

Angela said the first signs occurred during a December 8, 2020, visit when Maggie and Maggie's daughter, Andrea, came from Queens to Angela's Essex County salon for an appointment, followed by a friendly dinner.

Once the salon work was finished, the trio went to Moonshine in Millburn, N.J., just blocks from Angela's shop.

"We were sitting at the table and having drinks and a bit to eat and she reached a certain level, a level of concentration," Angela recalls. "Carol came to her and [Carol] started speaking and saying she wanted to go home and she was afraid and crying."

At one point, Maggie became too upset and loud to stay in the restaurant, prompting the three of them to head outside. "We had to leave so we walked out and asked if she was okay."

They walked Maggie to her car and as they helped her get in, she passed out and Andrea had to catch her. "Then about 20 seconds later she woke up and said 'What are you doing?' She had not remembered anything about leaving the restaurant."

What she did recall were the strong pleas from Carol that she return home and that her mother had worried about her, likely a sign of the night she died.

Maggie and her daughter left the location and returned home, both a bit shaken but believing this had been a stronger connection than usual and it would not go away without some action on her part.

A week later, Maggie and Andrea were back, stopping at Angela's house about five miles west of Millburn for a visit. Soon, the three joined another friend of Angela's and decided to go out for a bite and a drink.

This time they chose the Texas Roadhouse, a barbecue joint on busy Route 22 in North Plainfield.

"We were laughing and carrying on and she had a tall beer in front of her," Angela said about Maggie. "She was fine. Then she started laughing almost to the point of crying. She got very uncomfortable and said Carol showed up again and she wanted to go home."

Angela and the other companions quickly took notice and focused on what Maggie was doing, and [needing]. She was feeling the apparent Carol influence stronger than ever.

"She started saying, 'I want to go home, I just want to go home, take me home, take me to Jefferson," Angela said, repeating Maggie's words, which referenced Carol and Cynthia's childhood home on Jefferson Avenue in Maplewood. "She told me not to go with Mr. Nilson, saying 'Gail told me not to go.' She was upset that her parents would be worrying. 'I have to see my mother,' she kept saying."

They all left the bar as Maggie remained in her trance and claimed to be speaking for Carol, or more specifically that Carol was speaking through her. They carefully got into a car and headed east on Route 22 toward Maplewood.

Inside the vehicle, Andrea held on to her mother as Angela drove and their fourth passenger watched in amazement.

"We got in the car and Maggie kept talking. She was saying 'don't take me on Valley Street, don't take me on Valley. I have to go home,'" Angela explained. "We were trying to calm her down but it was not like it was her and there was a look of fear on her face. It was so obvious that she was in it."

The car continued down the highway with Maggie spouting Carol's apparent directions and concerns, nearly screaming at some moments and begging to be taken home, the same home she had been walking to the night she died.

The car exited the highway at Meisel Avenue in Springfield, taking a quick turn north on that street that would lead into Maplewood and toward Jefferson Avenue. Andrea held her mother's hand as Angela drove quickly and carefully and their fourth friend scanned the street ahead watching for obstacles.

"I want to go home. I need to get home, home to mom," Maggie kept uttering. "She is so worried, she needs to see me. I should not have gotten in the car."

The wind blew cold outside as the vehicle passed the street decorations of Springfield and Millburn, with picture window displays of holiday characters and gifts for sale zipping by.

The three women did not notice many of the Christmas-themed items on the street and in the shops as Maggie's trance continued. Once in Maplewood, Angela could not help but take a straight route down Valley Street, which led directly to Jefferson and Carol's one-time home.

When Angela pulled up in front of the house, Maggie said simply: "It looks so different, is this my house?" Told that it was, she passed out there in the backseat. The three others sat silent.

It was 8:30 p.m., the exact time that Carol's body had been found about a mile away 54 years earlier.

When Maggie awoke a few minutes later, she had not remembered anything about the trip but said Carol had been put to rest, she had found her calm.

"She said it was done, that she was okay now," Angela said. "All she wanted to do was to complete her destination, she just wanted to go home and this brought her home."

Adds Maggie: "I feel she is at rest, at peace."

Chapter Seventeen

There is a strong likelihood that the person who killed Carol Ann Farino was someone with whom she felt comfortable, but perhaps did not know so well. A customer from Milt's Cup & Saucer or George's Luncheonette, or some other entity in Maplewood Village where she was last seen.

Experts who spoke to me about the case indicate the probable assailant had seen Carol that night or knew where and when she worked.

By their own account, police found no evidence of any friends or acquaintances showing ties to the killing. They seemed to have targeted Frank Farino almost obsessively, but to no avail other than stressing him and his family for years.

No, Carol Ann Farino died at the hands of someone who came upon her from Maplewood Village as she took that long walk home. Someone who might have had a twisted affection for her, but also a dark, sadistic need to destroy her.

It may well have been Otto Neil Nilson. It may have been another semi-regular at Milt's or George's. Or perhaps a stranger off the train that night.

Based on evidence, expert views, and even a medium's insight, here is the most likely scenario and chain of events that led to Carol's murder.

The night Carol Ann Farino died, Maplewood Village was busy with the Democratic Party fundraiser at the Maplewood Theater and youngsters out and about with two days off from school. Weather reports for the day showed a clear evening ahead, but cold with temperatures in the 30s.

Still, a night off is a night off, and, as noted earlier, Carol's classmates were gathering for at least one party while others hit the usual nighttime hangouts and meeting places.

A chilly night also brought more customers to Milt's and George's, many likely seeking a warm place for dinner or a cup of cocoa or coffee. Carol would be busier than usual running from table to table, with one eye on the orders and another on the clock awaiting the end of her shift.

As usual, however, she was friendly and smiling to the patrons, many of whom were regulars, but undoubtedly several who came in now and then or had gotten off the train across the street for a first-time visit.

Workers at nearby shops along with cab drivers frequented Milt's and George's, some with unsavory records and reputations, while others were as harmless as children and just enjoyed a gregarious young server.

Carol's classic beauty and inviting grin would raise any customer's spirits. Sporting her classic white, tight-fitting uniform, the young woman was a lovely image, as well as a sexual object for the most decadent of male observers.

Add to that a gregarious personality, much needed in waitressing for the maximum tips, and it's no surprise that she was likely flirted with often.

And given her friendly nature and genuine interest in others, Carol would flirt back, too. Harmless and humorous, her interactions brought many regulars back again and again, not just for Milt's great coffee, but for his waitress's great rapport.

At least one customer Carol served that night took an extra interest in her. Someone who had seen her before and even watched as she would leave and head north on Maplewood Avenue toward her house.

Or maybe he spotted his prey later when she stopped at George's Luncheonette to grab a soda and chat with her former boss there. Was it Otto Neil Nilson, who had been known to patronize Milt's and even chat with Carol about religion and other issues, according to her sister?

Nilson had an office at the time at 173 Maplewood Avenue (currently above a nail salon), where he would later move to when he split up with his wife. With Milt's across the street at 174 Maplewood Ave. (Now the site of Anthony Garubo's salon) and George's, just down the block at 153 Maplewood Ave, (the current home of Roman Gourmet pizza), both became regular stops for the accountant who would later be unsuccessfully tried for another similar murder and end up in a psychiatric hospital until his death.

Or it was some other voyeuristic suspect who might have been smitten in a way that went beyond an adoring stranger or grateful customer. Like most young attractive women, Carol was used to whistling and catcalls, especially from older, perhaps less-successful men.

On a dark, cold night when she was exhausted from work and other demands, it was not always a welcome intrusion, but she learned to tolerate it as part of the job. Carol had other things on her mind as well, hoping to hear from her boyfriend who promised to get in touch but never did.

After serving the last customer of her shift, Carol waved goodbye to Milt and the other workers, then headed into the chilly night air. The wind blew in her face as she opened the door out onto Maplewood Avenue, buttoned up her blue car coat and felt the crisp November night.

Turning right, she headed up the short incline of the main street toward the post office to drop off the utility bill Milt had asked her to mail on her way home.

Climbing the few steps to the front post office entrance, now closed, she pulled open the mailbox handle and dropped the envelope inside, then let go to hear it clang shut.

Turning around, the chilly wind hit her again and she thought twice about heading directly up Maplewood Avenue toward her home street. This night called for another place to warm up first. She darted across the street and opened the door into George's Luncheonette, her former workplace, where the owner, George Mouhtis, remained a friend.

He welcomed her with a smile and directed her to a place at the counter, drawing a soda from the fountain and placing it in front of her.

"Cold night?" George asked as Carol reached for the drink and slid it toward herself, smiling. "Freezing," she said. As she lifted the drink again Carol scanned the room. The place was about half full with some recognizable faces, but a few that were unknown.

She looked up at the clock behind the counter and out the window just as the wind whipped up some leaves and a couple rushed by to the theater. She chatted some more with George and one of the waitresses with whom she had worked in the past.

Peering out the front window onto the busy street scene, Carol debated internally whether to call her father for a ride. She knew he was likely sleeping after his overnight hours the previous evening and would be cranky and angry at having to venture out just to give a ride.

Her sister, Cynthia, was all of 11 years old at the time so she couldn't do anything for a ride, while Ann Farino had never learned to drive, which left her out of the equation.

Carol could just picture her father's face when her mother asked him to venture out and pick her up. He would take it out on Carol as well once he arrived and ushered her into the car, and all the way on the ride home she would hear it.

She did not need that kind of aggravation and guilt trip on this night.

None of her co-workers back at Milt's would be free to walk with her either and no cab or other transportation was a worthwhile option.

After about 30 minutes she couldn't put off heading out any longer even with the chilly weather that awaited her on the dark trek up Maplewood Avenue. She bid farewell to her former boss and co-workers and braced for the cold air on the other side of the door.

Stepping out as the door shut behind her, Carol turned left and ran quickly past the crowded movie theater entrance next door, clutching her purse and closing her coat tight against the cold.

Taking a deep breath, she stopped suddenly at the corner of Maplewood Avenue and Durand Road as a car flew by, the driver ignoring the stop sign and cutting a sharp right into town.

Standing there, antsy to get going, Carol took what would be her last look around Maplewood Village—the bustling train station across the street with a line of cars picking up returning commuters, and back down the avenue as the quaint village was laid out in an autumn evening image of whipping wind, cloudy sky and shades of moonlight from the edge of the horizon.

One sight she did not see was the figure of an older, larger man who had followed her from Milt's to George's and kept a look toward her the entire time. He had thought about entering George's behind her, but hesitated, instead stationing himself in the small park, Ricalton Square, across from the luncheonette.

Named for Maplewood's first schoolmaster, James Ricalton, the small patch of land was a central meeting spot for Christmas tree lightings, holiday sing-a-longs, and quiet meetings for eating or reading.

On this early November night, the square was nearly empty as the man sat down and waited, keeping an eye on Carol whom he had been attracted to since she first served him at Milt's months ago.

Her womanly smile, attractive uniform, and friendly demeanor had lured him into a dark place of lust and depravity, but also some hope for what he believed was affection.

Married for six years, Otto Nilson's relationship with his wife, Carole, had already shown cracks even as they raised their children and enjoyed a comfortable life in South Orange. Just a few years later, he would separate from her and move into an apartment next to his office.

After a half-hour of waiting, he had almost decided to leave when Carol exited the eatery and headed north. When she reached the corner and stopped, the man jumped up and hurried to his car, parked a half-block away.

Once there, he opened the door and got in, turned the key and the motor revved up. Backing the vehicle out, he glanced back and nearly hit someone crossing Maplewood Avenue, before shifting into drive and pressing the gas with a screech.

The car zoomed forward down Maplewood Avenue, away from Carol, and took a sharp right turn at the first corner onto Inwood Place, then a right onto Woodland Avenue, and again on Durand.

As he reached the corner of Durand and Maplewood Avenue, the man looked left and saw that Carol had crossed the street and continued up Maplewood Avenue toward her street, Jefferson Avenue, about a half-mile ahead. Once there, she just had to take a right and walk past a few houses to her home.

But this man had other plans.

He focused his eyes on the young, innocent object of his desire, and perhaps helpless frustration. He'd been watching her for weeks, both inside Milt's and out on the street. Each time she served him his favorite quick supper, that grin and an extra helping of friendliness added to his urging to make a move.

Several times he followed Carol from behind as she walked that route home and turned right on to her street. Not every night. As the fall temperatures had dropped, she would occasionally get a ride with a friend or co-worker or get a buddy to walk with her, making any move by the man impossible.

Just days ago he had even passed by her on her walk home and slowed down, almost about to stop, when he lost the nerve and drove on. But earlier this evening she seemed almost lonely, at least in his twisted view, and that gave him the belief that she might be approachable.

Carol had reached about 50 yards down Maplewood Avenue when he made his turn onto the street and slowly drove toward her. Carol was clearly cold and stopped to pull the coat tighter to block the chill, but then appeared to shiver again.

He chose that time to make his move, pulling a few feet ahead of her and over to the side as she stopped with surprise and then walked carefully up the sidewalk, both nervous and curious as to who this was.

Sliding over from the driver's side to the passenger side of the car, the man rolled down the window by hand and called out to his prey. "Excuse me, Carol, isn't your name Carol?" he said, recalling her name tag from so many visits to the diner. She hesitated, then smiled as she recognized him as a regular customer, although she never knew his name.

"Yes, hello," she said cautiously, then kept moving.

"You must be freezing. How about a ride?" the semi-stranger asked. "Do you live near here?" Having followed her home he knew exactly where her house was, but did not want her to know.

"Thanks, but I'm okay," she said. "My house isn't that far."

But the man smiled an impish grin and reached his hand out to take hers. Carol felt a warmth when he touched her and couldn't help but smile at his charm.

She had noticed him in the diner, an attractive older man. Even his quiet demeanor and slight helplessness drew her as someone who seemed safe simply by his familiarity.

And as the chill gripped her body, it seemed an even longer walk home at that moment and she gave in to the request, opening his car door, stepping into the front passenger seat, and slamming it shut.

"Thanks," she muttered and barely looked at her driver, choosing to look down at her hands, then ahead as if to remind herself that home was not too far off and it was probably okay to take his offer.

With slightly wrinkled dress pants, a buttoned-up short-sleeve shirt—complete with pens in the pocket—the man looked as if he had just come from the office. His wristwatch glowed with shiny gold and he stepped on the accelerator with shined black shoes.

Carol remained a bit guarded, pulling the edge of her dress uniform down over her knees and glancing up at the man to see what he was doing. His eyes stared straight ahead as he made small talk, trying to put his passenger at ease.

The teenager did not relax and watched the passing houses as she clutched the door tightly in an effort to feel safer. Each one meant she was closer to home and the safety zone of her room.

But when the driver passed Jefferson and kept going, she felt a shiver down her back.

"I think you missed it," she said. "My house was a right on Jefferson."

"Oh, sorry," he responded, "I'll take the next right and go around the block."

That would be Parker Avenue, which ran parallel to Jefferson and was where Columbia High School was located. He took a sharp right there and headed toward Valley Street.

But as Carol expected him to take another right on to Valley, and then later onto Jefferson, he began to slow down as he approached one of the high school parking lots.

The school had two large lots about a block from the CHS building, one for seniors and the other for any visitors. The senior lot was reserved and students were assigned spaces when they reached 12th grade, then given permits for use. No permit and you'd find a ticket after school.

The man turned right into the senior lot, then drove to the back area farthest from the street and close to the railroad tracks. Carol's shiver turned into a frightening shake as he turned the car off and shut out the headlights.

"Wait, what are you doing?" she shrieked. "Wait, no, what do you want?

Take me home!" Her hand immediately went for the door lock and the handle on her side, but he grabbed her left arm and pulled her toward him.

"It's okay," he said calmly. "I'm not going to hurt you. I just want to get a kiss."

The man held her arm tighter and pulled her other shoulder around so she faced him. Carol began to shake and kept asking him to stop, tears streaming down her face.

"No, I don't want to, let me go," she yelled. Then she started to scream: "Help! Help!" But the words fell on deaf ears as a train roared by and shook the car with noise.

As he drew her closer she resisted, pulling her head back away from his and struggling to break free. He jerked her close, then kissed her on the lips, but she snapped back and wiggled from his grasp.

Carol grabbed for the car door, but the man pulled her again and slapped her face, sparking her to cry. "Damn it!" he said. "I wanted to be nice about this."

With that, she struggled further and cried more, then the terror of the moment took her over and she screamed: "Help me! help me!" But the pleas could not be heard with the car doors shut and the nearest house at least two hundred feet away.

The assailant held her down and climbed onto her knees, facing her as he put his hands on her upper arms to hold her in place. He felt his twisted rush of power and lust, but also a conflicting sense of guilt and some strange affection.

He liked this girl and thought she liked him. She'd been kind to him, served him and he even led him on—or so his delusional mind wanted to think.

Other women, even his wife, would not provide the kind of youthful allure that a teen girl brought, mixed with her courteous behavior and attentiveness. She was just doing her job, but he took it as more in a weird rationalization mixed with sociopathic roots.

"What are you going to do?" Carol said in a moment of calm, her face reddened from fear and tears still streaming. "Don't hurt me, please! Let me go." He held her tighter and shook his head: "I won't hurt you if you help me."

Then he went in to kiss her and she closed her eyes, recoiling back. Just as he was going to touch his lips to hers she spat at him.

The man jumped back, both in surprise and hurt at being rejected. But then anger took over and he slapped her again. As Carol began to cry he popped, moving off of her lap and pulling up her uniform skirt. She fought back, trying to pull her clothes back down over her knees but he won the battle and raised the skirt up.

He formed a sick smile seeing her undergarments and pulled at her girdle while unsnapping the hooks to her stockings and managing to pull them off.

Carol screamed again just as another train passed by, muffling her sound. She was there with her girdle down and her stockings off, but her body still held tight. Just then, the man went to unbutton his pants and let go of her for a moment.

That's when she made a move.

Pulling herself up from the seat she pushed her knee hard into his groin, then punched him in the chest. He grabbed at his genitals and winced in pain. That freed her a bit more and she kicked him there again, this time with her shoe.

The attacker winced again and fell sideways, still clutching her stocking and closing his eyes with shock and pain.

This was her chance to escape, she thought, and grabbed for the door.

But it was locked and she frantically went for the lock, only to find his hand clutching her fingers before she got hold of it.

Still angered at the pain, he knew he could not perform the act he had wanted to, forcing sex on her, and grew even angrier.

"Please let me go," Carol begged again and began to cry. But the man felt a wave of anger stronger than before and wanted to take it out on her.

He held her by the throat and pressed her neck and head into the seat, cutting off her air supply and causing her to gag. He pushed so hard the back of the car seat broke and the two of them fell backwards into the rear seat area, almost at a horizontal angle.

Realizing he still had the stocking in his other hand, he wrapped it around her neck and pulled it tight, gripping it like a hog-tied animal rope.

Carol gasped further, kicking and grabbing at the stocking and even trying to scratch his eyes out, but it was no use. Tears streamed down her face as she realized what was happening and she grew white. Slowly her kicks were weaker and her eyes closed as life was taken from her 17-year-old body.

Then the friendly, generous young waitress who exhibited kindness, intelligence, and warmth, who friends said would not hurt anyone and adults described as a model teen, laid there a lifeless object taken too soon and in a way that would rival the worst kind of undeserved torture.

Her killer let go of the stocking and began to shiver himself. He suddenly realized what he had done and almost teared up. But the sociopathic personality that had led him to this moment remained. He felt slight guilt and helplessness, but more instant wonder at how to get out of this situation.

Whatever regard he had for the woman he had killed, he had more concern for his self-interest and how to get away undetected. Looking around the empty, dark, cold parking lot, the man made sure no one had seen anything and went into the back seat. Since the front passenger seat had been shifted back, Carol's body was halfway in the back anyway. So he pulled her completely back, pushed the seat up again, and laid her on the backseat floor.

He went to the trunk and took out a blanket, then covered her body with it and got back in the driver's seat. Starting the engine, he looked around again and saw no one had noticed him or come by.

Stepping on the gas pedal, he steered back toward Parker Avenue and turned right onto the street. Then he stopped at the red light on Valley Street, just at the corner of the high school, and turned right again.

A strange calm overtook the murderer as he steered along Valley Street and passed Memorial Park, the same place Carol and many other teens would gather regularly and where many were congregating at that moment.

As he drove he felt less and less remorse and more settled in what he had done, almost convincing his twisted mind that he had to kill her and that it would be the right thing.

In the back seat, down on the dirty, stinking car floor like an old shoe or a rotting piece of food lay Carol Ann Farino. A vibrant, positive, hopeful young woman just minutes earlier. This twisted animal had taken her life from her, as well as from her family, and, of course, her sister.

Passing Maplewood Town Hall and, eventually, the Maplewood Country

Club, the killer's mind raced at what to do. His first thought was getting rid of the body of this life he had just destroyed.

But where? And how?

He made sure to keep from surpassing the speed limit to avoid being pulled over. How would that be: killing someone without being seen and then getting caught from a speeding ticket?

As he saw the red light of busy Millburn Avenue way ahead in the distance, he realized he could not stay on the main roads and looked for a side street. He cut left in a quick turn onto the first one he saw, then steered up the hill of what he'd later find was Sommer Avenue. Quieter than Valley Street, but still too noticeable.

Looking from side to side at the passing homes, the man decided he was still too out in the open to drop Carol's body here and continued to head up. Then the signpost for Hubert Place on the right caught his eye. He turned slowly and scanned the area, even checking behind his car. It was much darker, shorter, and quieter than the other streets.

Halfway down the road, he saw the garage and driveway for 22 Sommer, which faced Hubert and was far removed from the house via a patio. That meant it was a good distance from the residents who might otherwise hear or see him.

He pulled over to the right slowly, at the edge of the driveway, and got out. Going to the passenger side backdoor, he opened it quietly and pulled the blanket off Carol.

The sudden shock of seeing her face, eyes open but lifeless, made him wince. Looking both ways and behind him, he pulled her body out and carried it to the driveway, laying it under a tree near the back by the garage. Once he put her down, her body slid a bit, causing him to reach down and pull her closer to the tree, in an effort to reposition her.

He walked quickly back to the car to shut the back door, looking around once again. Then he noticed the blue car coat still in the front seat. e grabbed it and threw it toward the driveway where it landed at the edge of the asphalt.

The killer refused to look again at what only minutes before was a lively, beautiful, and kind young woman, a snuffed-out existence that had been full of life, promise, and hope.

The murderer got into the front driver seat, shifted the car into drive, pressed the gas, and began moving forward. As he gained speed on Hubert Place, then halted for the stop sign, he glanced in the rearview mirror, making sure no one was behind him.

Then he turned right, hit the gas again and he was gone.

Coda

The chance that Carol Ann Farino's death will ever be solved remains slim. After nearly 55 years, her killer is probably deceased himself, and the blockades to further investigation among the Maplewood Police Department and the Essex County Prosecutor's Office appear strong.

Neither law enforcement agency seems willing to re-open the case with any real effort or new mission to solve it and give Cynthia Farino some kind of justice, satisfaction, or closure.

Hell, they won't even let her see what they've been doing about her sister's murder for the past 50 years. And barring some potential high-cost legal challenge, they may never do so.

Still, I believe we have brought many of the issues and evidence to light and shown that the most likely known killer is Otto Neil Nilson. The troubled man who was accused in another case, although acquitted, and later sent away to a mental hospital for a violent attack had opportunity, personality, and no known alibi.

And at least one respected cold-case solving medium touted him as the most believable assailant. Both of these facts have convinced Cynthia of his probable involvement.

"I think it is solved, for all intents and purposes, I think what Maggie said makes the most sense," Cynthia told me in early 2021 as this book's editing took place.

But unless and until any official decision or finding of his or anyone else's guilt is determined, the mystery will continue. "That they say it is an open case is outrageous," she said.

The U.S. Justice Department estimates there are at least 250,000 unsolved murders in the nation, according to a 2019 report, with another 6,000 added each year. And many date back further than 1966.

So Carol and her surviving sibling are not alone.

"Cold cases constitute a crisis situation, for all unsolved homicides potentially have offenders who have never been apprehended," Tom McAndrew, an expert on the Justice Department's Cold Case Investigation Working Group, said in the report. "History and research show that a violent offender will likely repeat."

Research indicates Nilson was someone with a history of crime, and at least one murderous accusation. But even if it was not him, perhaps Cottingham or one of the other potential suspects, all of them were tied to multiple illegal acts.

Meanwhile, Cynthia Farino remains the last link to Carol's life and death and a vital voice for information to be found that will solve it. She is strong and hopeful in her small Jersey Shore house, joined by her only roommate, a cat named Shopper.

During the months of research that involved hours of interviews and conversations, Cynthia was incredibly forthcoming and open—about Carol's life and death, but also about her own struggles and experiences and how they were directly affected by having a sister murdered.

As an 11-year-old, she felt the impact in many ways for the next 50 years, and even today.

Cynthia says she has found at least some solace in believing who killed Carol and in learning more about what happened and how others viewed her sister. But she said it never leaves her thoughts.

"I am so immersed in this I think about her every day, all the time especially after that episode where they had to take her home," she said, referring to Maggie's wild ride for Carol. "I was on the phone listening to the whole thing, the first time she went into a trance. It was very upsetting."

And then there is Cynthia's rollercoaster ride of a life. She finally found a man who loved and cared for her after so many troubled relationships, and she was able to keep that love going for more than 20 years before Michael passed away.

But baggage from other men and experiences will always linger.

"I don't want to spend the rest of my life alone, but I don't want to get married again," Cynthia said. "I don't want to go through that again, what happened with Michael and watch someone get sick and die."

Seeing her sister die so young, her parents lose their lives after such a long, bitter marriage, and then her husband's demise can't help but leave her with mixed feelings.

But she does not regret her lack of children. She saw parenting somewhat through Michael's offspring, but never wanted to take on the responsibility. "I decided very young I never wanted to have kids, I don't know why. Everything that happened soured me on it. My parents, what happened to Carol, I did not want to take a chance on that."

As for the future? "I don't know where I'm going right now," she said in early 2021.

Cynthia Farino has asked that if anyone wishes to offer information or clues related to her sister's death they may contact her at the following post office box:

C. Herman
P.O. Box 35
Atlantic Highlands, NJ 07716

About the Author

Joe Strupp is an award-winning journalist with 30 years' experience spanning newspapers, magazines, radio, television, cable and the web. He spent 18 years covering media and news issues for *Editor & Publisher* magazine and Media Matters for America.

He spent eight years in San Francisco during the 1990's covering city and political topics for *The Independent*, a citywide newspaper that covered all aspects of the City by the Bay.

Joe's work has also appeared in *Salon.com*, *San Francisco* magazine, *MediaWeek* and *New Jersey Monthly*. He has received honors from the New Jersey Press Association, Society of Professional Journalists, Syracuse University's Mirror Awards, The Jesse H. Neal Business Journalism Awards and Folio.

Joe is currently a reporter at the *Asbury Park Press* in New Jersey, a freelance writer and adjunct professor in media at Fairleigh Dickinson University and Rutgers University. He is also the author of *The Crookedest Street* (a novel) and *Killing Journalism: How Greed, Laziness (and Donald Trump) Are Destroying News and How We Can Save It*.

Joe lives in New Jersey with his wife, Claire, and his children, Cloey and Cole.

Also by Joe Strupp

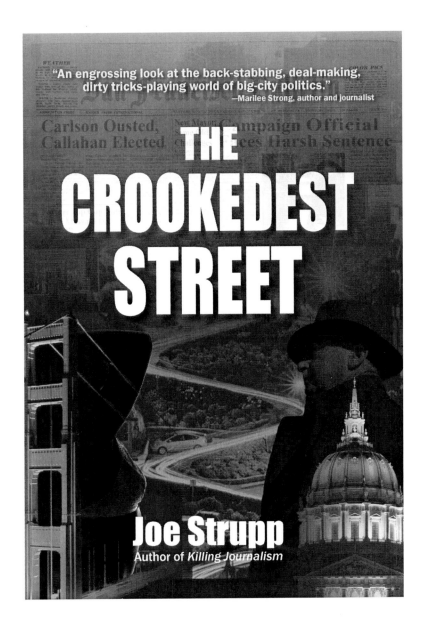

"An engrossing look at the back-stabbing, deal-making, dirty tricks-playing world of big-city politics."
—Marilee Strong, author and journalist

THE CROOKEDEST STREET

Carlson Ousted, Callahan Elected

Campaign Official Faces Harsh Sentence

Joe Strupp
Author of *Killing Journalism*

Available online or through your local bookseller.

Made in United States
North Haven, CT
31 October 2021